KFK KINGFISHER KNOWLEDGE

EPIDEMICS & PLAGUES

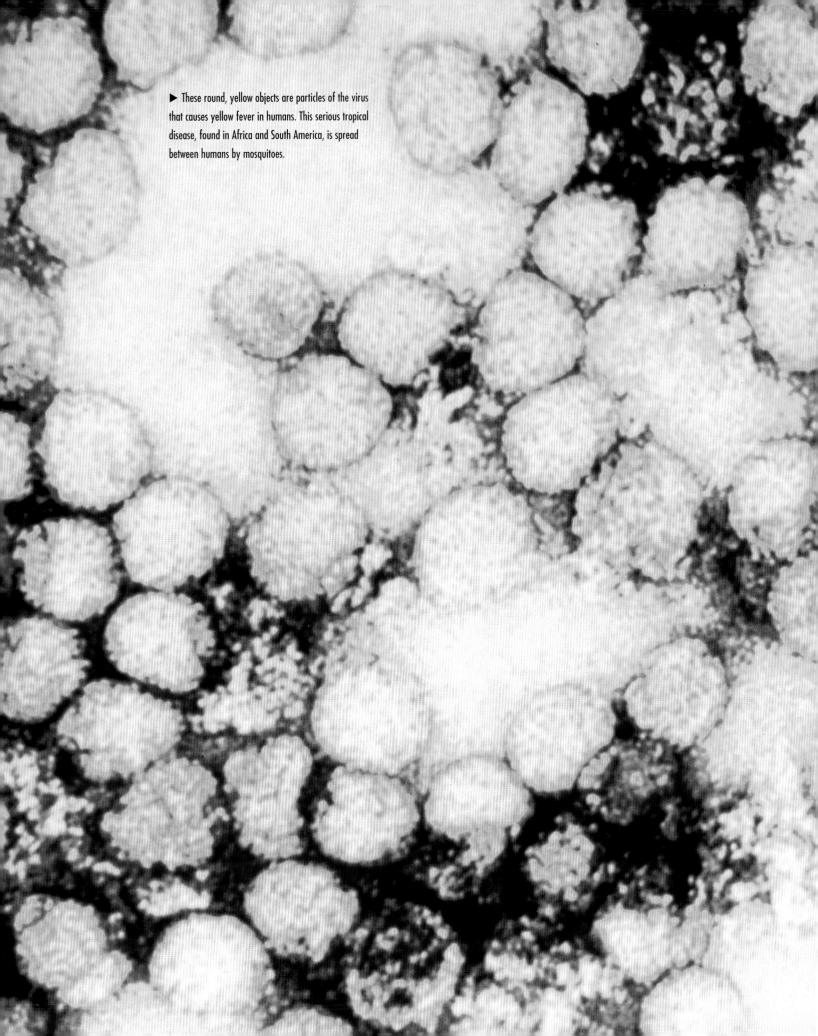

► These round, yellow objects are particles of the virus that causes yellow fever in humans. This serious tropical disease, found in Africa and South America, is spread between humans by mosquitoes.

EPIDEMICS & PLAGUES

Richard Walker

Foreword by
Denise Grady

KINGFISHER

Editor: Marie Greenwood
Designer: Rebecca Painter
Consultant: Dr Geoff Watts
Picture research manager: Cee Weston-Baker
Picture research: Pernilla Nissen
Senior production controller: Lindsey Scott
DTP manager: Nicky Studdart
Indexer: Alan Thatcher

KINGFISHER
Kingfisher Publications Plc,
New Penderel House,
283–288 High Holborn, London WC1V 7HZ
www.kingfisherpub.com

First published by Kingfisher Publications Plc 2006
10 9 8 7 6 5 4 3 2 1

1TR/0706/TWP/MA(MA)/130ENSOMA/F

ISBN-13: 978 0 7534 1376 0
ISBN-10: 0 7534 1376 0

NOTE TO READERS
The website addresses listed in this book are correct at the time of going to print.
However, due to the ever-changing nature of the internet, website addresses and
content can change. Websites can contain links that are unsuitable for children.
The publisher cannot be held responsible for changes in website addresses or
content, or for information obtained through third-party websites. We strongly
advise that internet searches should be supervised by an adult.

GO FURTHER...
INFORMATION PANEL KEY:

websites and
further reading

career paths

places to visit

Contents

▼ This photo was taken in Chicago, USA, in 1956, during a polio epidemic. Parents and children wait outside an emergency vaccination centre to receive their vaccination against the disease, which can cause paralysis. Polio vaccination trials were only completed in 1955.

Foreword

Humans are a remarkable species. We think, speak, read and write. We invent aeroplanes and computers, decode our own genes, and create medicines to prevent and cure illness. Surely we are the masters of our destiny, cleverly shaping the environment to suit our needs? Well… yes and no. To a surprising and humbling degree, human history has been shaped by invisible enemies, the micro-organisms responsible for the epidemics and plagues described in this book. These life forms are minute, but still manage to wreak havoc in our world. Disease is a force of nature, a powerful one that has spurred human migrations and helped decide the outcome of wars and the fates and fortunes of individuals and nations.

Yellow fever ravaged the army that Napoleon sent to Haiti in 1802 to suppress a slave rebellion there. France lost thousands of soldiers to the disease. Haiti won the war, and its independence. In the 1890s, the same disease killed so many people working on the Panama Canal that building had to stop. Not until the disease was brought under control could the canal be finished – by the USA, in 1914.

Today, infectious diseases are still a formidable threat, despite vaccines that prevent them and drugs that treat them. As a journalist who writes about medicine and health, I have witnessed at close-hand the emergence of new diseases that have appeared without warning.

In 1981, as reporters began to write about unusual infections that were turning up in New York and California, USA, none of us realized we were witnessing the birth of a new disease, AIDS, that would become a devastating worldwide epidemic, killing 20 million people by 2006. Today, millions of people are infected with the AIDS virus, and although drugs can keep it in check, many of the hardest hit countries cannot afford the medicines. In Africa, the disease has made orphans of 12 million children, and in some African countries it has wiped out much of the workforce. Scientists have yet to create a vaccine.

Livestock diseases have battered the economies of some countries, forcing them to destroy millions of animals to keep the infections from spreading to humans. Hong Kong wiped out its entire poultry population in 1997 to keep bird flu from spreading, and the UK destroyed more than 100,000 cattle because of fears about the brain disease BSE.

Bird flu remains a lingering menace: despite efforts to stamp it out, it has advanced steadily around the world, from Asia to Europe to Africa. The disease has led to the deaths of tens of millions of birds, either killing them directly or by leading health officials to destroy them in the hope of halting outbreaks. The virus does not spread easily to people or between them, and so human cases, by comparison, are rare. But when bird flu does jump to people it is uncommonly lethal, killing at least half its known victims. If the disease becomes more contagious, and easily transmissible among people, it could turn into a worldwide epidemic that would kill millions of people.

Fears of deadly, global flu have led to a flurry of preparations in many countries. But even as they worry about avian flu, health officials know that the next epidemic may well come from another source, one they could not have even begun to imagine.

Denise Grady, science reporter, *The New York Times*

CHAPTER 1

Death and disease

For thousands of years, humans lived in groups, their survival dependent on foraging for plants and hunting animals. If a disease arose it might kill some or all of the group, but would spread no further. Then people started to settle in order to farm the land. Settlements grew into cities, good news for disease-causing micro-organisms, or pathogens, that could therefore spread rapidly and infect more people. These widespread outbreaks of disease, or epidemics, devastated communities and changed history. Epidemics were first seen as divine retribution or plagues sent by God to punish people for their sins. Only more recently have we come to understand the causes and how to control them. But while less of a threat in the West, infectious diseases are still the major cause of death in the developing world.

In this 15th-century illustration, passers-by shy away from those who have died from epidemic disease.

▲ A plague of a different kind was described in the Bible, and still afflicts parts of the world, such as Africa, today. Usually after heavy rains, when crops are guaranteed to produce good harvests, swarms of desert locusts devour crops and leave people starving.

First epidemics

Around 11,000 years ago, people's way of life changed. Some of our hunter-gatherer ancestors swapped their nomadic life for a more settled life as farmers. Much later, agriculture would support settlements called towns and cities. An unforeseen consequence of settlement was an increase in human diseases, and with that the first epidemics.

Farmers and town-dwellers

When early farmers domesticated ('tamed') animals for meat, milk and skins or wool, diseases spread from animals to their keepers, giving rise to new infections, such as measles and smallpox. These diseases flourished in the first towns and cities that appeared around 5,000 years ago. For the first time large numbers of people lived close together, providing ideal conditions for epidemics and plagues – outbreaks of disease that spread quickly and affect, and often kill, many people.

▲ This southern European woman tends her flock just as people have done since sheep, cattle and goats were first domesticated around 9000BCE. Domestication meant that, for the first time, animals and humans lived close together. This allowed animal pathogens (micro-organisms) to 'jump' to people. Some of these caused new epidemic diseases in humans.

▲ In this 3,500-year-old Egyptian carved stele (stone slab), the man leaning on a staff has a withered leg. This suggests that he has suffered from polio, a highly contagious viral disease, which can cause paralysis and muscle wasting. In ancient towns, polio spread rapidly in water contaminated by virus-laden faeces.

Ancient evidence

How do we know whether ancient civilizations were afflicted by epidemics? Clues provided by historical objects such as sculptures and paintings suggest that epidemic diseases such as smallpox, polio, typhoid and typhus were widespread. In the Bible's Old Testament, the book of Exodus describes the ten plagues inflicted upon the Egyptians for failing to liberate the Israelites. Whether factually true or symbolic, the story reflects how human societies were vulnerable to epidemics.

Plague in Athens

Around 429BCE, during the Peloponnesian War between the city-states of Athens and Sparta, a plague spread through Athens. As the Spartans laid siege to the city, disease wiped out one-third of its population. Among the victims was Pericles, a great Athenian statesman. The 'Golden Age' of Athens was now at an end. After centuries of speculation, in 2006 Greek scientists identified typhoid as being a likely cause of the plague of ancient Athens.

▲ The construction of the Parthenon – the temple to Athene – on the Acropolis in Athens was masterminded by Pericles (493–429BCE). This charismatic Athenian leader died when an epidemic – probably of typhoid – spread rapidly through his besieged and overcrowded city.

Powerful pathogens

Until the middle of the 19th century, it was widely believed that infectious diseases were caused by mysterious vapours, dirt, or even stagnant water. It took the work of two brilliant scientists – Louis Pasteur and Robert Koch – to prove that disease-causing micro-organisms, called pathogens or germs, were the real culprits. We know now that the major pathogens are viruses, and certain types of bacteria and protists.

Germ theory

Bacteria were first discovered in the 17th century, but their link to disease was not recognized. Then, in the 1860s, pioneering French scientist Louis Pasteur (1822–95) showed that bacteria cause disease. Robert Koch went further by showing that certain pathogens cause particular diseases. Between them Pasteur and Koch established the Germ Theory of Disease – that each infectious disease is caused by a specific bacterium or other micro-organisms. This discovery was to change medicine forever.

▶ German doctor and pioneer bacteriologist Robert Koch (1843–1910) is shown here at work in his laboratory. Koch developed techniques to culture, or grow, bacteria. He became the first scientist to identify that certain bacteria caused specific diseases, including TB (see pages 38–39). For his work he was awarded the Nobel Prize in 1905.

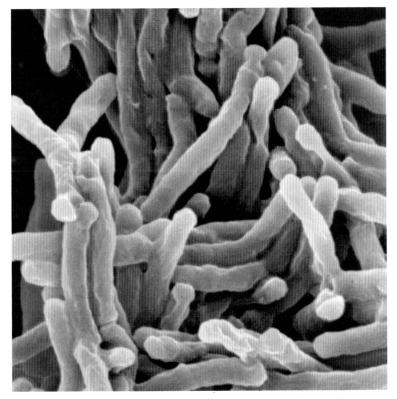

▲ Bacteria can be spherical, spiral-shaped, or rod-shaped like these 0.002mm-long *Mycobacterium bacilli*. *Mycobacterium* causes the lung disease TB and is spread by droplets of watery mucus.

Viruses

Far tinier than bacteria, viruses are non-living pathogens that neither feed nor grow. Each virus is a chemical 'package' consisting of genetic instructions surrounded by a protein coat. To 'reproduce', a virus invades and hijacks a living cell, forcing it to make lots of new viruses that break out of the host cell – often damaging or killing it – before invading other cells. Diseases caused by viruses include colds, flu, measles, mumps and rubella.

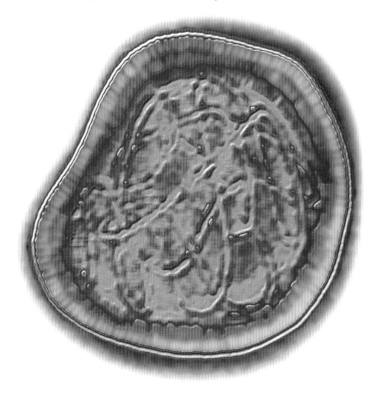

▲ Just 0.00007mm across, this rubella (German measles) virus has a protein coat (yellow) surrounding genetic material (red). Spread by airborne droplets, rubella causes a rash.

Bacteria

The smallest and most abundant of all living things, bacteria are found almost everywhere. Each individual bacterium consists of a single, simple cell. Most bacteria are harmless, including those that live on our skin. But some – commonly known as 'germs' – are pathogens. Once inside the body, if not intercepted by the body's defences, they can multiply rapidly, and release poisons called toxins that damage cells or alter body processes. Serious bacterial diseases include cholera, diphtheria, whooping cough, typhoid and TB (tuberculosis).

Protists

These single-celled organisms are bigger than bacteria, and have complex cells rather similar to those of animals and plants. Most, such as the familiar shape-changing amoeba and tiny green algae, are harmless, living freely in soil and water. But around 30 protist species cause diseases in humans. These include malaria and sleeping sickness, both serious illnesses that are spread by insects and affect millions of people in tropical areas.

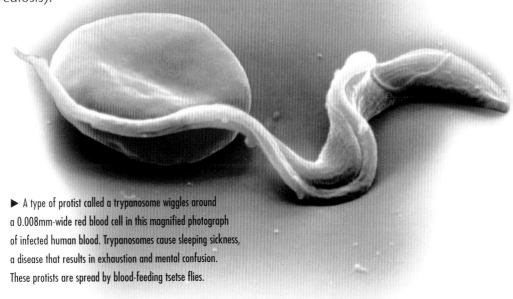

▶ A type of protist called a trypanosome wiggles around a 0.008mm-wide red blood cell in this magnified photograph of infected human blood. Trypanosomes cause sleeping sickness, a disease that results in exhaustion and mental confusion. These protists are spread by blood-feeding tsetse flies.

◀ High-speed photography captures the moment when a woman sneezes. Tiny droplets of water and mucus, that may be carrying viruses, spread out into the surrounding air at speeds of up to 150km/h.

▼ A busy subway train is an ideal place to pick up pathogens. People may catch them by breathing in infected droplets that have been coughed or sneezed into the air, or by holding on to poles or handles smeared with infected mucus, then touching their mouth, nose or eyes.

Person to person

Infectious or contagious diseases are caused by pathogens. But how do these pathogens get from one person to another? Some infectious diseases are caught through direct or indirect contact. Others are transferred through the air or are found in contaminated food or water. A few are transmitted by animals. Knowing how diseases spread is vital when controlling epidemics.

Through the air

Whenever we sneeze, cough, or even talk or laugh, we send a spray of tiny droplets of watery mucus into the air. These droplets may contain pathogens that, if breathed in by another person, could make them ill. This is how colds and measles spread. When infected droplets dry out they float like dust particles. These too can spread disease if they carry pathogens – such as those that cause flu, whooping cough or TB – that can survive in dry conditions.

Direct and indirect contact

Direct contact involves the transfer of germs from infected to uninfected people by touch (through infected skin or cuts) or kissing (through saliva). This usually happens between close friends or family members. Indirect contact happens when an infected person holds or sneezes over a surface such as a door knob or phone, leaving behind pathogens. When an uninfected person touches the object, then touches their mouth, nose or eyes, those pathogens can enter their body.

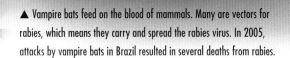

▲ Vampire bats feed on the blood of mammals. Many are vectors for rabies, which means they carry and spread the rabies virus. In 2005, attacks by vampire bats in Brazil resulted in several deaths from rabies.

Through a vector

Animals that are capable of transmitting diseases to humans are known as vectors. These include ticks, flies, mosquitoes, bugs, rats, dogs and bats. The most harmful vectors are female mosquitoes. They penetrate the skin to feed on blood, at the same time injecting pathogens in their saliva. Diseases spread by mosquitoes include malaria, West Nile virus, dengue fever and yellow fever. Other vector-spread diseases include Lyme disease, transmitted by ticks, and rabies, spread by dogs and bats.

▲ Never mix cooked meat with raw meat, as shown here. Bacteria on the uncooked food can infect the cooked products, which, when eaten without further cooking, will cause food poisoning. Harmful bacteria can also be spread by a person who goes to the toilet, does not wash their hands, then touches cooked food.

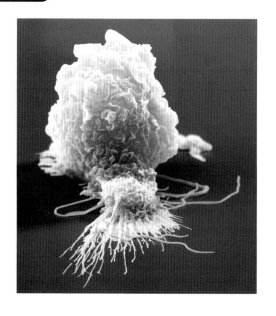

◀ Having hunted down several invading *Borrelia* bacteria (blue strings), a macrophage (yellow) sets about destroying them. Different types of *Borrelia* bacteria cause several diseases in humans including Lyme disease. The devouring macrophage sends out extensions that grab the bacteria then pull them inside it to be digested.

Body defences

All the time, we are threatened by pathogens that, given the opportunity, invade our body and cause disease. Luckily, the body has a series of defences against this. First, barriers such as skin halt their progress. Next, the immune system launches its counter-attack. Pathogen-eating phagocytes spring into action, and lymphocytes release their germ-disabling antibodies. If all these fail, medical help is at hand.

Germ eaters

Any pathogens that manage to breach the body's outer defences – such as the germ-proof skin – face tough opponents called neutrophils and macrophages. Both of these are phagocytes – germ-eating white blood cells that are attracted by invading pathogens, just like a bloodhound following a scent. At the site of infection they leave the bloodstream to hunt down their prey. Once contact is made, neutrophils, and the bigger, more powerful macrophages, swallow up pathogens and digest them.

2. When Y-shaped antibodies bind to antigens on the bacterium (green) they disable it.

1. A lymphocyte (blue) releases Y-shaped antibodies (yellow) that target a specific invading bacterium.

▲ When pathogens, such as these bacteria, invade the body they are identified by the antigens or markers that project from their surface. Once a pathogen is identified, a group of lymphocytes start making and releasing antibodies that will bind to that specific pathogen's antigens. Antibodies halt the pathogen's activities and make it tastier for passing phagocytes.

Immunity and vaccination

The immune system's white blood cells, called lymphocytes, identify specific pathogens then target them with disabling chemicals called antibodies. Lymphocytes also 'remember' an intruder, responding even faster if it invades again. This process gives us immunity to a disease. Vaccination by a doctor introduces a fragment or a weakened version of a life-threatening pathogen – such as the diphtheria bacterium – into the body. This means the immune system will recognize and speedily destroy the 'real' pathogen if it should invade.

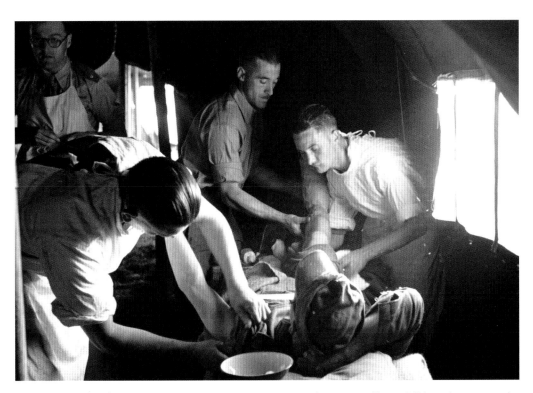

▲ Army doctors in a World War II field hospital treat an injured soldier. As part of his treatment the patient is given the antibiotic penicillin to reduce the risk of infection. Before World War II, more soldiers died from wound infection than in battle.

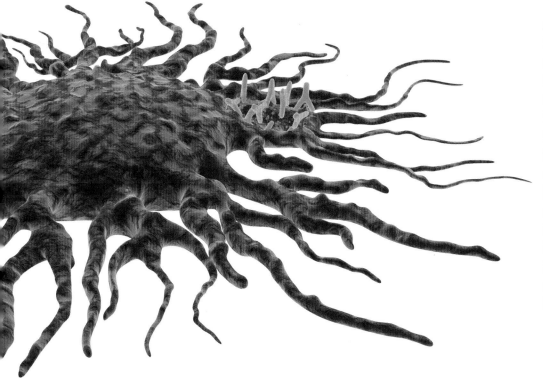

3. A macrophage (pink) sends out extensions that engulf the marked bacteria, then digest them.

Antibiotics

Before the mid-20th century, bacterial diseases and the infection of wounds by bacteria were major causes of death. In 1928, Scottish medical bacteriologist Alexander Fleming (1881–1955) discovered penicillin, the first antibiotic, a drug that could disable or kill bacteria. In production by the early 1940s, penicillin saved millions of lives during World War II. Many other life-saving antibiotics have been discovered or made since then. Unfortunately, bacteria can develop resistance to antibiotics, allowing infections such as MRSA to flourish.

Disease detectives

In the 1800s, scientists made the connection between micro-organisms and infectious disease. Since then, researchers have looked into the causes and transmission of diseases in populations. These disease detectives, or epidemiologists, investigate how existing diseases spread, the sources of epidemics, and what is behind new diseases. Here are some examples of their work.

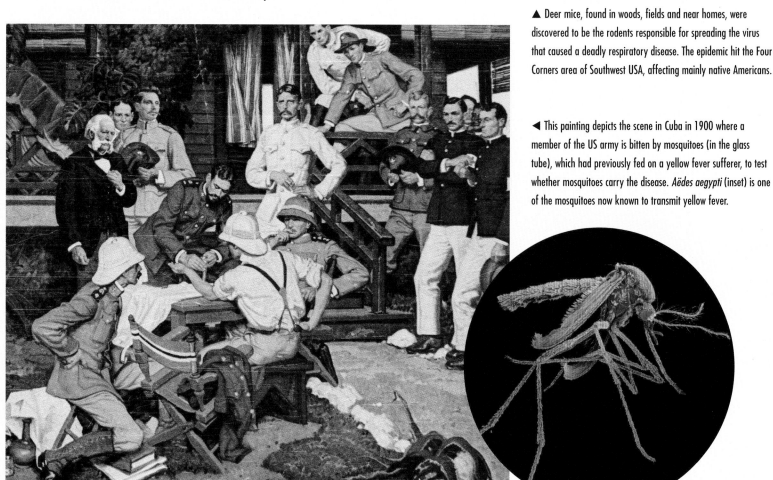

▲ Deer mice, found in woods, fields and near homes, were discovered to be the rodents responsible for spreading the virus that caused a deadly respiratory disease. The epidemic hit the Four Corners area of Southwest USA, affecting mainly native Americans.

◀ This painting depicts the scene in Cuba in 1900 where a member of the US army is bitten by mosquitoes (in the glass tube), which had previously fed on a yellow fever sufferer, to test whether mosquitoes carry the disease. *Aëdes aegypti* (inset) is one of the mosquitoes now known to transmit yellow fever.

Yellow fever

Causing fever, bleeding and coma, yellow fever killed thousands in the Americas between the 1600s and 1800s. How it spread was unknown. In 1900, a US army team in Cuba tested the theory that mosquitoes were responsible. By carefully designed experiments, in which healthy volunteers were given bites by mosquitoes that had fed on yellow fever sufferers, the team proved that mosquitoes were the vectors, or carriers, of the disease.

Mystery disease

In 1993, in the USA's Southwest, a deadly epidemic broke out. The mystery disease caused breathing problems before killing its victims. A combination of epidemiology and the knowledge of Navajo elders showed that the disease was caused by viruses breathed in from the dried droppings of deer mice. That year, the deer mouse population had grown because heavy rainfall had greatly increased the crop of piñon nuts, their favourite food.

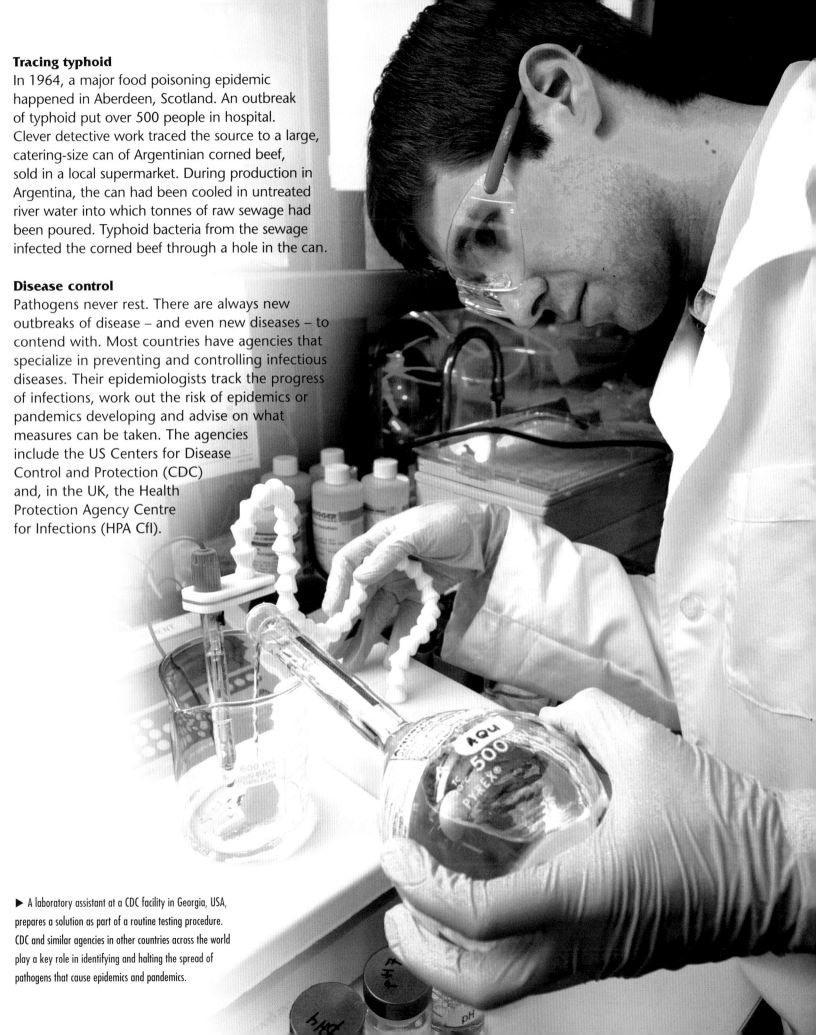

Tracing typhoid

In 1964, a major food poisoning epidemic happened in Aberdeen, Scotland. An outbreak of typhoid put over 500 people in hospital. Clever detective work traced the source to a large, catering-size can of Argentinian corned beef, sold in a local supermarket. During production in Argentina, the can had been cooled in untreated river water into which tonnes of raw sewage had been poured. Typhoid bacteria from the sewage infected the corned beef through a hole in the can.

Disease control

Pathogens never rest. There are always new outbreaks of disease – and even new diseases – to contend with. Most countries have agencies that specialize in preventing and controlling infectious diseases. Their epidemiologists track the progress of infections, work out the risk of epidemics or pandemics developing and advise on what measures can be taken. The agencies include the US Centers for Disease Control and Protection (CDC) and, in the UK, the Health Protection Agency Centre for Infections (HPA CfI).

▶ A laboratory assistant at a CDC facility in Georgia, USA, prepares a solution as part of a routine testing procedure. CDC and similar agencies in other countries across the world play a key role in identifying and halting the spread of pathogens that cause epidemics and pandemics.

Childhood diseases

The figures say it all. In prosperous Sweden 0.3 per cent of children die before the age of five. In Sierra Leone, 6,000km away in Africa, it is 28 per cent. Today, 99 per cent of children who die before they are five live in developing countries. Most deaths are due to easily preventable diseases, such as diarrhoea and measles. Meanwhile, in the developed world, childhood death is largely eliminated by vaccination and better public health.

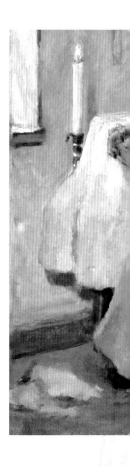

▶ This 19th-century portrait shows the death of a child. In the 1800s there were no vaccination programmes and public health was poor. As a result, childhood death was so common, it was a 'normal' part of family life.

Deadly water

In some parts of the world clean drinking water is taken for granted. But in many others, dirty water, often contaminated with sewage containing pathogens, causes hundreds of thousands of cases of diarrhoea in children every week. Untreated, diarrhoea will severely dehydrate (dry out) a child's body. Dehydration resulting from diarrhoea is one of the biggest killers of children in the developing world. Clean water for all would solve the problem.

◀ A girl in southern Asia collects water to carry home for her family, a journey that might take several hours. This water, coming from a tap, should be clean, but from other sources, such as wells or lakes, the water could be contaminated with pathogens that cause several types of stomach upsets.

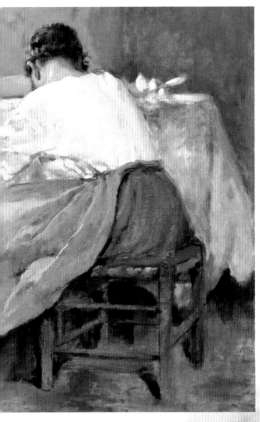

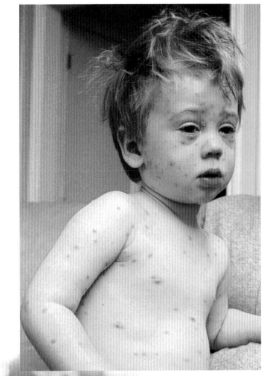

▶ This child has measles, a viral disease that produces flu-like symptoms and a skin rash. Measles is highly contagious, spreads in droplets through sneezes and coughs, and can be fatal, especially when children are malnourished.

Measles today

Measles is the childhood disease most easily prevented by vaccination. In the West, where most children survive the disease unharmed, vaccination has reduced cases to a trickle. But in the developing world the disease kills nearly 500,000 children annually. The good news is that the Measles Initiative – set up in 2001 by major health organizations – aims to reduce deaths by 90 per cent by 2010. By December 2005 it had already vaccinated 200 million children in 40 countries, saving an estimated one million lives.

Beating polio

Highly contagious, and passed on in contaminated water, polio viruses cause fever and stiffness, and possibly paralysis. Routine vaccination has banished polio epidemics from the developed world, but elsewhere it is still a problem. However, polio may have met its match. The Global Polio Eradication Initiative (GPEI) vaccinates millions of vulnerable children every year. In 1988, when GPEI was established, polio was endemic (constantly present) in 125 countries and 1,000 children were paralysed daily. In 2005 there were 1,906 cases, and the disease was endemic in just four countries.

▶ On his way to school, an Indian boy who has had polio leans on his sister for support. He is unfortunate in being one of a small proportion of polio sufferers who develop paralysis and muscle wasting. His right leg is supported by a brace.

Bad eating

The word 'epidemic' is not just used to describe infectious diseases. It is often used to illustrate a widespread problem, such as malnutrition. Literally meaning 'bad eating', malnutrition might take the form of a shortage of vital nutrients such as vitamins or a lack of clean drinking water. In contrast, another type of 'bad eating' – that of eating too much junk food – has led to an epidemic of obesity.

▼ In the Philippines, International Rice Research Institute scientist Sophan Datta holds a variety of 'golden rice'. These rice plants have been specially developed so that they contain orange-yellow beta-carotene, a substance converted by the body to vitamin A.

Missing vitamins

In the past, sea voyages of exploration were risky ventures, and not just because of shipwrecks and piracy. At sea for months, many sailors developed scurvy, a disease that caused bleeding gums and loose teeth. Ship's doctor James Lind suspected scurvy was caused by the sailors' poor diet. In 1747 he tested his idea with a designed experiment. He selected 12 sailors with scurvy, divided them into pairs, then gave each pair different diet supplements. But only one – oranges and lemons – cured scurvy.

▲ James Lind (1716–94) examines one of the 12 sailors taking part in his clinical trial to find a cure for the disease scurvy. Lind showed that citrus fruits, such as oranges, limes and lemons, prevented scurvy, a disease shown much later to be caused by a lack of vitamin C.

▲ Bangladeshi women collect water from one of millions of tube wells that should have brought their country clean water. In fact, many wells were contaminated with poisonous arsenic.

Golden rice

Around 150 years after Lind's experiment, scientists first demonstrated that diseases such as scurvy are caused by a lack of vitamins. Vitamin deficiency diseases are still widespread in the developing world. For example, every year around 350,000 pre-school children go blind due to vitamin A deficiency, because rice, a major part of their diet, lacks the vitamin. However, science may have found one part of the answer. A strain of rice that does supply vitamin A – called golden rice – has been developed.

Poisoned water

Essential for life, the water we drink should be free of the pathogens that cause vomiting and diarrhoea. Until the mid-1970s, most people living in Bangladesh, southern Asia, lacked clean water supplies. Then some 10 million tube wells were dug, providing 97 per cent of the population with germ-free water. But years later, the well water was found to be contaminated with arsenic, resulting in the biggest outbreak of mass poisoning in human history.

◄ An overweight teenager plays soccer with his friends. The developed world is experiencing a slightly different malnutrition epidemic – obesity among adults and children. The epidemic has resulted from people eating too much fat- and sugar-laden food, which is bad for their health.

Famine and blight

Epidemic diseases that affect humans often have serious effects. But so too can diseases that attack vital crops and livestock. Throughout history such diseases have had lasting impacts on human societies. Three examples are described here. The Irish potato blight changed Ireland's history forever. Coffee rust, another fungal disease, changed a nation's drinking habits. And viral rinderpest continues to threaten domestic cattle in Africa and Asia.

Irish potato famine

In the 1840s, many people in Ireland lived in poverty, surviving mainly on a diet of potatoes. But in September 1845, potato plants across Ireland were infected with the fungus *Phytophthera infestans*. The resulting potato blight caused plants to blacken and potatoes to rot into mush. Over the next five years famine devastated Ireland. More than a million people died and many more emigrated to the USA and elsewhere.

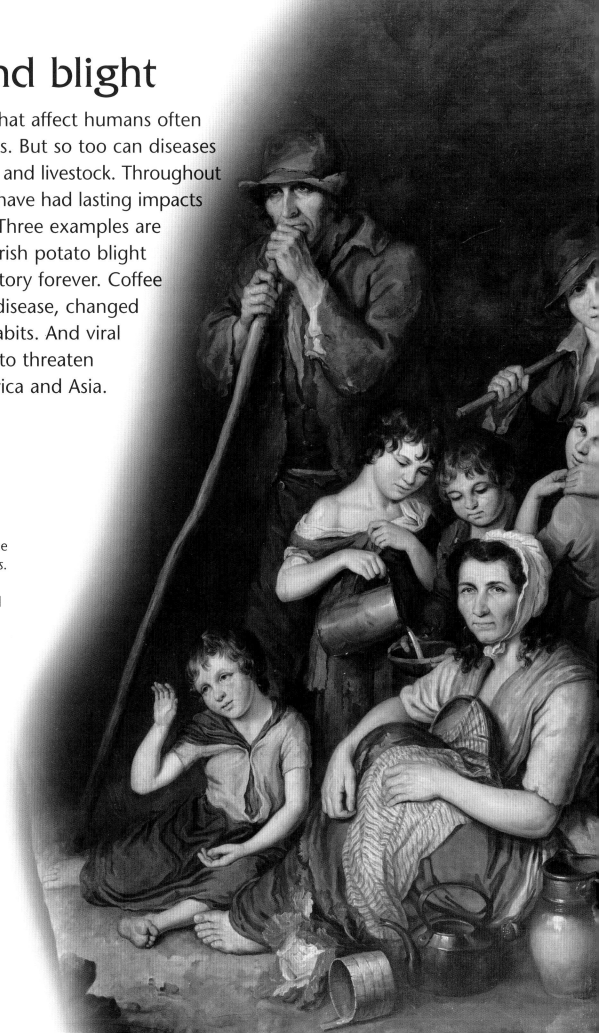

▶ The look of desperation on the faces of this Irish family is obvious. Tired, hungry and malnourished, their lives, and those of millions of others, were devastated by the famine that struck Ireland during the 1840s.

Coffee rust fungus

The British are known around the world as tea-drinkers, but this was not always the case. In the 1800s, coffee was more popular, and Sri Lanka – then the British colony of Ceylon – was the world's largest producer of coffee beans. But in the 1870s and 1880s, coffee rust fungus, which kills coffee plants, spread across Sri Lanka. In response, growers replanted not with coffee but with tea plants, and tea became the favourite drink of the British.

Rinderpest

Meaning 'cattle plague' in German, rinderpest is a highly contagious, usually deadly, viral disease that has ravaged cattle, domestic buffalo and other livestock in Asia and Africa for centuries. In societies that depend on cattle for food, rinderpest epidemics cause famine and poverty. In the 1890s, rinderpest wiped out 90 per cent of all cattle in sub-Saharan Africa. Today, the Global Rinderpest Eradication Program aims to eliminate the disease by 2010.

▼ A Maasai herdsman tends his cattle. For the Maasai people of East Africa, cattle are vitally important, representing wealth, power and food. By killing most of their cattle, the rinderpest outbreak of the 1890s wiped out the Maasai's resources at a stroke.

▲ Women harvest leaves from tea bushes in Sri Lanka. From minor beginnings – a single plantation established in 1869 – tea exports from Sri Lanka to other countries now exceed 300,000 tonnes each year.

SUMMARY OF CHAPTER 1: DEATH AND DISEASE

This blood-feeding tsetse fly transmits sleeping sickness to humans.

Earliest epidemics

It was in the Middle East, around 9000–8000BCE, that farming first began. Living in close proximity to their animals, early farmers picked up diseases from them. Later, when people established towns and cities, these diseases spread rapidly and affected many, causing the earliest epidemics. Polio, smallpox, typhus and plague were just a few of the diseases that killed many people and altered the course of history.

Causes and defences

The real causes of infectious diseases became apparent in the 19th century through the work of Louis Pasteur and Robert Koch. Their Germ Theory demonstrated the link between a disease and a particular pathogen. In order for disease to spread, pathogens have to pass from one person to another. Transfer may be through breathed-out droplets, direct or indirect contact, or by animal vectors that carry and spread disease. The relentless assault by invading pathogens would soon overcome the human body were it not for the built-in defences that protect us 24 hours a day. These defences are boosted by vaccination and, when they fail, by antibiotics and other germ-killing drugs. The discovery of the links between germs and disease in the 19th century established epidemiology, the study of the sources of epidemics and how they spread.

Epidemics in action

While epidemics are far less common in the West than they were a century ago, they are still a major cause of death in the developing world. Hardest hit are children, especially the under-fives, who die in their millions from diseases that are readily curable. The word 'epidemic' is also used today to describe problems, such as childhood obesity, that affect many people world-wide. Finally, epidemics may not affect people directly – an epidemic of fungal potato blight, for example, in 1840s Ireland resulted in famine, death and mass emigration.

Go further...

Follow the 'Immune Platoon', meet today's epidemiologists... and lots more at:
www.bam.gov/sub_diseases/index.html

Explore the world of diseases by going to the Epidemic website at:
www.amnh.org/exhibitions/epidemic/index.html

Horrible Science – Deadly Diseases by Nick Arnold (Scholastic Hippo, 2000)

Kingfisher Knowledge: Microscopic Life by Richard Walker (Kingfisher, 2004)

Bacteriologist
Studies bacteria.

Immunologist
Scientist or doctor who studies the immune system and the use of vaccines.

Medical microbiologist
Scientist who identifies pathogens and advises on how to control their spread.

Physician
Doctor who treats disease by methods other than surgery.

Virologist
Studies viruses, their infection techniques, and the diseases they cause.

Discover more about Germ Theory and Louis Pasteur's work by visiting:
Musée Pasteur,
25, rue du Docteur Roux,
75015 Paris, France
Telephone: +33 (0)1 45 68 82 83
www.pasteur.fr/pasteur/musees/museesUS/pasteur/visite.html

To find out more about the work of CDC visit:
Tom Harkin Global Communications Center Exhibit Area,
Centers for Disease Control and Prevention,
1600 Clifton Road, N.E. Atlanta, Georgia 30333, USA
Tel: +1 404 639 0830
www.cdc.gov/gcc/page.do

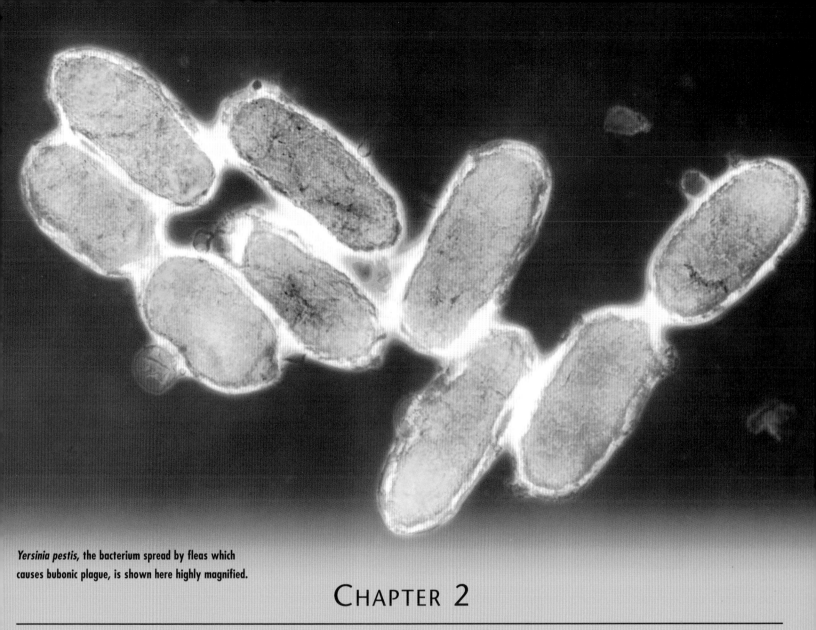

Yersinia pestis, the bacterium spread by fleas which causes bubonic plague, is shown here highly magnified.

CHAPTER 2

Plagues and pestilence

To people living today the threat of an epidemic is frightening. But imagine how it felt for people in earlier times who had no understanding of diseases and how they spread. For thousands of years, plagues and pestilence cut swathes through populations, killing millions. Terrified by the unknown, people saw these devastating diseases as punishment from God. 'Plague' is a term often used to describe any deadly and contagious disease, but specifically it refers to bubonic plague, a disease that devastated Europe in the 14th century CE. Other terrible and often fatal diseases – known as pestilences – afflicted the medieval world. This was a time when explorers and traders started to travel widely. As they did so, they spread diseases further, creating widespread epidemics or pandemics.

The Black Death

Between 1347 and 1351, a deadly plague that became known as the Black Death spread like wildfire across Europe. Its name derives from the black swellings found on many of its victims, most of whom died in agonizing pain. The worst pandemic ever known, the Black Death killed at least 25 million Europeans – over one third of the population – and changed the lives of those who survived.

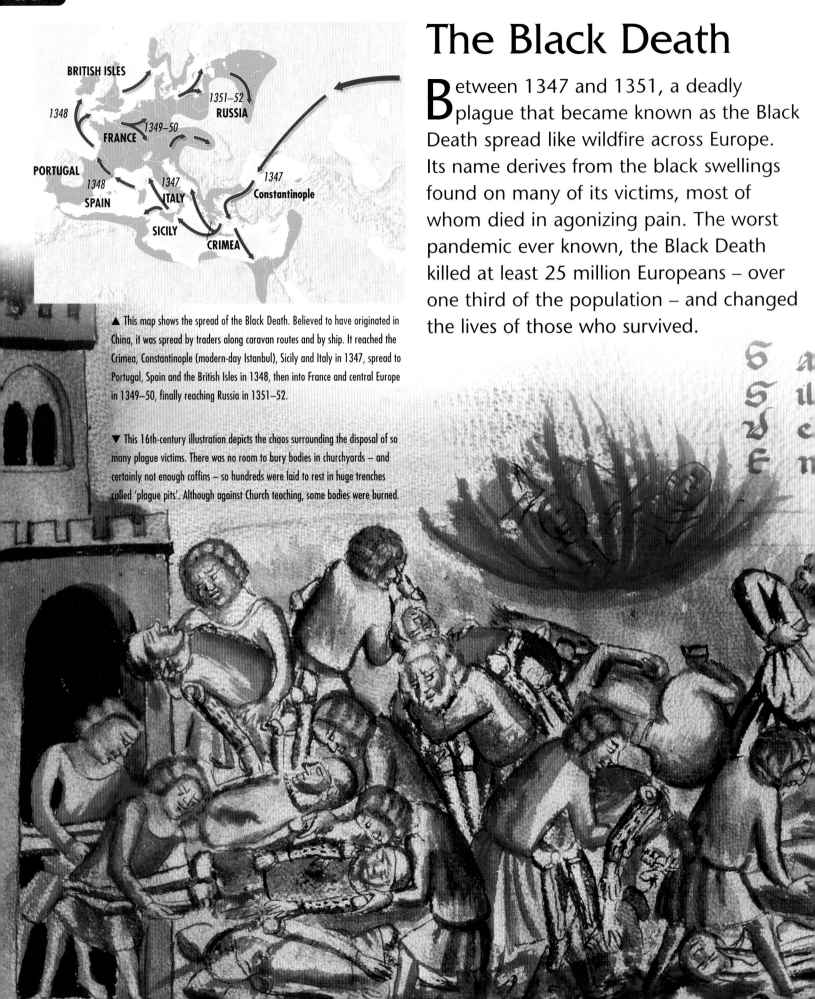

BRITISH ISLES

1351–52

RUSSIA

1348

1349–50

FRANCE

PORTUGAL

1348

1347

SPAIN

ITALY

1347

Constantinople

SICILY

CRIMEA

▲ This map shows the spread of the Black Death. Believed to have originated in China, it was spread by traders along caravan routes and by ship. It reached the Crimea, Constantinople (modern-day Istanbul), Sicily and Italy in 1347, spread to Portugal, Spain and the British Isles in 1348, then into France and central Europe in 1349–50, finally reaching Russia in 1351–52.

▼ This 16th-century illustration depicts the chaos surrounding the disposal of so many plague victims. There was no room to bury bodies in churchyards – and certainly not enough coffins – so hundreds were laid to rest in huge trenches called 'plague pits'. Although against Church teaching, some bodies were burned.

Symptoms and causes

Those struck down by the Black Death suffered pain, fever and black tumours in the groin and armpits. People vomited blood and their skin became blackened due to internal bleeding. Death occurred within a day or days, and recovery was rare. It has long been accepted that the Black Death was bubonic plague, a bacterial disease spread by rat fleas. But in 2001, two British scientists suggested that, because the Black Death spread so rapidly, it might have been caused by a virus similar to present-day Ebola (see page 56) that passed directly from person to person.

Social change

Whatever its cause, the Black Death changed society forever. The feudal system – in which serfs or peasants worked a small parcel of land and paid taxes in the form of food or service to a lord – crumbled. The massive death toll produced a shortage of skilled workers, allowing surviving serfs, who had been treated like slaves, to demand wages for their labour. The newly awakened hopes of downtrodden serfs led to uprisings such as the Peasants' Revolt in England in 1381.

▲ Bubonic plague – so-called because of the buboes, or swellings, it produces – is caused by the bacterium *Yersinia pestis* (identified in 1894) which infects the black rat (*Rattus rattus*) and other rodents. It spreads to people when a rat flea *Xenopsylla cheopis* (inset) feeds on the blood of an infected rat and then on a human.

Retribution and blame

Bewildered, terrified and panicked by this unknown and bizarre disease, people had little idea what was causing so many to die so hideously. Some saw it as divine retribution, punishment from God for the sins of mankind. Others tried to blame other people, such as lepers. Many sought protection through talismans (lucky charms), potions, self-punishment for sins committed, or other – as we now know – useless methods. In fact, the cause of the plague remained a mystery for centuries.

▶ This 13th-century illustration shows a serf and his pigs. Serfs existed at the lowest level of the feudal system. They worked the land, providing food and labour for their landlord in return for his protection. In turn the landlord provided services for his knight, the knight for his baron, and the baron for his king, who owned the land. The Black Death triggered an end to this system.

Medieval sickness

Plague was only one of many pestilences, or diseases, that blighted people's lives in medieval times. Their causes unknown, these pestilences were seen as a punishment for wickedness or blamed on the unfavourable movements of the planets. Most, such as St Anthony's fire (now called ergotism), leprosy and king's evil, are today understood and curable. But others, including sweating sickness, remain a mystery.

▲ This ear (the seed-carrying part) of rye is infected with the ergot fungus *Claviceps purpurea* (brown). Rye, like wheat, is a cereal grass whose seeds can be ground to make flour.

St Anthony's fire

People suffering from St Anthony's fire experienced burning sensations (hence the name) and hallucinations, 'danced' crazily and developed gangrene. The deadly disease caused widespread fear and sufferers were often condemned as witches. In the 17th century, the cause was found to be chemicals released by the fungus ergot, which grows on damp rye and contaminates the flour used to make rye bread.

Leprosy

In 13th-century Europe, leprosy reached epidemic proportions, and at that time it was incurable. Sufferers were considered 'unclean' and were shunned. The disease, now known to be bacterial, produced skin sores, numbness and disfigurement. It was considered, wrongly, to be highly contagious, and sufferers were forced to live in isolated colonies outside city walls. By the 15th century, the disease had all but disappeared in Europe.

▶ This 14th-century illustration shows leprosy sufferers, their bodies covered with sores. They are being tended by Franciscan monks, members of the order established by St. Francis of Assisi who taught that lepers were as deserving of care as anyone else.

Sweating sickness

Also called *sudor anglicus* (English sweat), sweating sickness first appeared after the Battle of Bosworth Field in England in 1485. This serious epidemic disease caused terrible sweating, breathing problems, convulsions and, usually, death. It spread rapidly, affected mainly young, fit men, both rich and poor, and killed quickly – a person taken ill at midday could be dead by evening. There were several outbreaks in the 16th century which spread across Europe, but the disease disappeared in 1551. Its cause remains unknown.

▶ During the Battle of Bosworth Field, knights of Henry Tudor – soon to become King Henry VII (reigned 1485–1509) – and the doomed King Richard III (reigned 1483–85) fight to the death. Henry's army of French mercenaries may have brought sweating sickness to England from mainland Europe.

King's evil

Scrofula, or king's evil, has afflicted people since ancient times. It is now known to be a type of tuberculosis (TB) that infects and enlarges lymph nodes in the neck and can cause disfigurement. It gets its alternative name of king's evil from the supposed ability of royalty to cure the disease by touching the sufferer. This practice continued up to the 1700s. Now rare, the disease is treated using antibiotics.

▼ In an attempt to cure him, England's Queen Anne (reigned 1702–14) administers the Royal Touch to 12-year-old scrofula sufferer Samuel Johnson (1700–84), later a famous writer and critic. The disease left his face deeply scarred.

The Great Pox

Between 1493 and 1494 a devastating new disease – called the Great Pox – broke out in the southern Italian city of Naples. The disease – later called syphilis – spread rapidly, transmitted from person to person by sexual contact. Initially syphilis caused pain, terrible disfigurement and rapid death. In time, however, the disease changed to the more slowly advancing, still potentially fatal, form found today. Syphilis remained incurable until the 20th century.

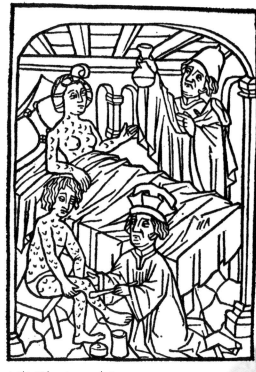

▲ This 16th-century woodcut shows a man and woman with syphilis being attended by two doctors. In its original form the disease produced sores, disfigurement and an early, painful death. By the 17th century the nature of the disease had changed.

Origins and spread

Some people argue that explorer Christopher Columbus (1451–1506) and his crews brought the Great Pox to Naples from the Americas. Others believe the disease emerged in Naples and was caused by a new, dangerous form of *Treponema pallidum*, the bacterium now known to cause syphilis. Whatever its origins, syphilis spread rapidly across Europe as French king Charles VIII's troops, infected with the disease while occupying Naples, fled after being defeated in 1495. Early sufferers had hideous sores and rotting flesh, but gradually syphilis changed in form.

▲ The French king Charles VIII (1470–98) pictured during his doomed campaign in 1494–95 to capture Naples, where the first outbreak of syphilis had just occurred.

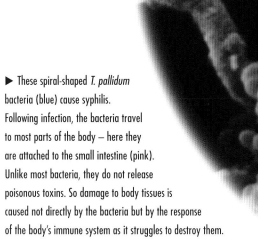

▶ These spiral-shaped *T. pallidum* bacteria (blue) cause syphilis. Following infection, the bacteria travel to most parts of the body – here they are attached to the small intestine (pink). Unlike most bacteria, they do not release poisonous toxins. So damage to body tissues is caused not directly by the bacteria but by the response of the body's immune system as it struggles to destroy them.

Symptoms and sufferers

Left untreated, syphilis has three stages. First, painless sores appear which later go of their own accord. Then there is a rash and fever, from which the person recovers. Finally, up to 50 years after infection (the bacteria never leave the body) the disease damages many organs including the brain. This results in dementia (memory loss) and can cause death. Many famous people in history have had syphilis, including England's King Henry VIII, Austrian composer Franz Schubert and Spanish artist Francisco Goya.

▶ Possibly maddened by the final stage of syphilis, which damages the brain, Russia's first tsar, Ivan 'the Terrible' (1530–84), was responsible for the violent deaths of thousands of his subjects, including his own son.

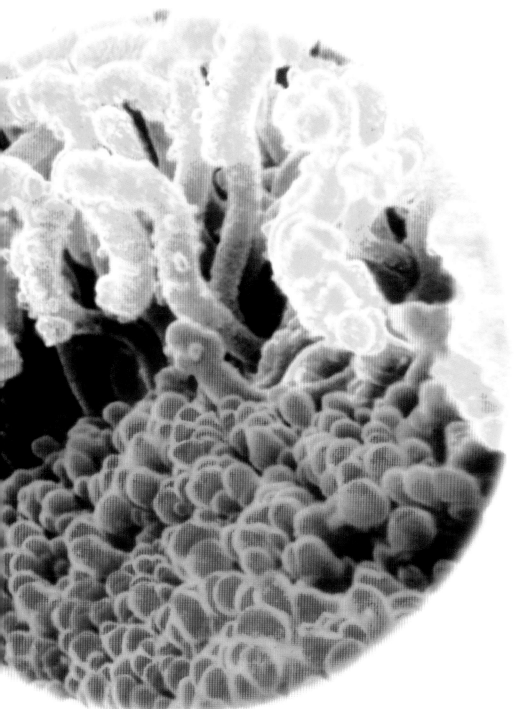

Beating syphilis

Until the 20th century the only treatment for syphilis was mercury, which poisoned the bacteria but also risked killing the patient. In 1910, German chemist Paul Ehrlich (1854–1915) developed Salvarsan, the first bacteria-killing drug. Salvarsan had limited use against syphilis, unlike the antibiotic penicillin, which from 1943 caused the number of syphilis cases to plummet. Today, the number of sufferers is increasing again. However, in 1998 the DNA make-up of the bacterium *Treponema pallidum* was analysed. This may pave the way for new treatments for the disease.

Vulnerable to attack

The ancestors of today's native Americans migrated about 12,000–15,000 years ago across a land bridge that linked Siberia in eastern Asia to Alaska in North America during the last Ice Age. When the Ice Age ended, the bridge disappeared. Now isolated, these migrants and their descendants were never exposed to epidemic diseases such as smallpox and measles that appeared in Europe and Asia. Until, that is, European explorers arrived in the Americas. Lacking any immunity (resistance to infection), between 90 and 95 per cent of native Americans were killed by imported diseases.

▲ All that remains of the once great Inca empire are items such as this gold mask from Peru dedicated to the Sun god Inti. Like other native Americans, many Incas were killed by diseases to which they had no immunity.

Conquistadors

In the 16th century, invading Spanish and Portuguese explorers and soldiers – known as *conquistadors* ('conquerors') – brought much of the Americas under their control. Ancient civilizations, such as the Aztecs of Mexico and the Incas of Peru, were destroyed and their peoples killed in the fighting, and, more significantly, by the diseases that the *conquistadors* carried, as they plundered their lands for gold, silver and diamonds.

Spreading smallpox

Also called the 'speckled monster', deadly smallpox cut through native populations in the Americas. In some cases epidemics may have been started deliberately. It was suggested, for example, that Lord Jeffrey Amherst – commander of British troops in North America 1754–1763 – ordered that native Americans be given blankets used and infected by smallpox victims. With no natural immunity to smallpox, the native population was wiped out.

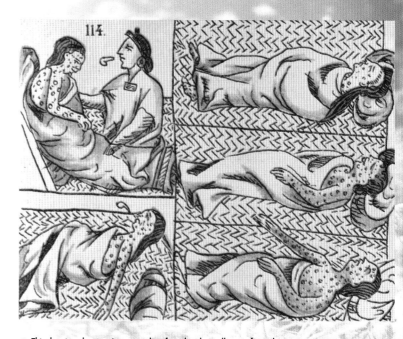

▲ This drawing showing Aztec people infected with smallpox is from the *General History of New Spain* published between 1547 and 1569. The book describes the Spanish conquest of Mexico (the 'New Spain') through Aztec eyes.

Still vunerable

There are still parts of the world – such as the tropical forests of Papua New Guinea and the Amazon basin – where hunter-gatherers live isolated from the outside world. Today their lives are threatened by illegal loggers and miners. As these people invade the forests in search of timber, gold and diamonds, they expose forest dwellers to diseases such as measles, chickenpox and influenza, to which these native peoples have no resistance.

▲ Painted in 1839 by Karl Bodmer (1809–93) this scene shows a funeral scaffold to a chief of the Sioux, one of the tribes of native North Americans. Thousands of Sioux died during a smallpox epidemic in 1837–38.

◀ A young man in Papua New Guinea hunts using a bow and arrow, a skill passed down from father to son for generations. Forest dwellers like him are at risk if exposed to diseases brought into the forests by outsiders.

Plague epidemics cropped up across Europe for centuries after the Black Death in the 1340s. The final outbreak of plague in England was the Great Plague of 1665. Worst hit was its capital city, London, although the disease affected other places too. Plague spread rapidly and killed quickly, its cause unknown. The sick were forcibly confined to their homes until they died or, less likely, recovered.

Plague's progress

The first cases occurred in May 1665. The plague's victims developed painful swellings, or buboes, in the groin and armpits before – usually – dying a painful death. The epidemic spread rapidly with 6,137 deaths in July, 17,036 in August and 31,159 in September. Some believed 'miasmas' or poisonous air spread the disease. Others blamed cats and dogs, many thousands of which were destroyed. This only made the problem worse, because without their natural predators the population of black rats increased.

Bring out your dead

Black rats harboured the fleas that, as was discovered later, carried the plague bacterium. When plague killed rats, their hungry fleas started feeding on, and infecting, humans instead. Houses containing plague victims were sealed and marked with a red cross. Paid 'searchers' called out 'Bring out your dead' and removed bodies for mass burial. In the summer heat, plague tore through London uncontrollably. In the winter cold it disappeared, never to return. But by then it had killed some 100,000 people.

Plague in Eyam

In August 1665, plague struck the Derbyshire village of Eyam. Its source was a box of flea-ridden cloth that had arrived from London. Local tailor George Viccars was the first to die, and others soon followed. Terrified, the villagers wanted to leave, but clergyman William Mompesson persuaded them to remain and isolate themselves to avoid spreading plague to neighbouring villages. They did not starve because people living nearby left food at Eyam's parish boundary. Their self-sacrifice meant that the disease did not spread into surrounding areas, but it was at a great cost to Eyam. By the time plague had run its course in October 1666, 260 of the 350 villagers who had remained were dead.

▲ Under cover of darkness, a searcher loads the bodies of the dead onto a cart to carry them to a plague pit for burial. Dead rats, also killed by plague, litter the filthy streets. To the left, a plague doctor wears robes, gloves and a beak-like mask filled with sweet-smelling flowers to protect him from the 'miasma' of diseased air. He visits patients but can do little to help.

▲ This detail from a window in the parish church of Eyam shows a dying man surrounded by neighbours who had volunteered to remain in their plague-ridden village in 1665–66.

SUMMARY OF CHAPTER 2: PLAGUES AND PESTILENCE

Dated 1400, this image shows a leper ringing a warning bell.

Devastating diseases

In 1347, a deadly plague pandemic arrived in Italy. It was called the Black Death, because of the painful black swellings that afflicted its victims. Over the next four years it spread to Europe's farthest corners, leaving around 25 million people dead in its wake. Its real cause unknown, the plague was seen by many as divine retribution, a punishment from God for their 'sins' and 'wickedness'. Only in the late 19th century was bubonic plague shown to be caused by a bacterium and spread by fleas carried by black rats. But plague was not the only pestilence to afflict medieval societies. Epidemics of St Anthony's fire (ergotism), leprosy, scrofula, sweating sickness (a disease yet to be identified), the Great Pox (syphilis), and other diseases struck without warning, leaving many of their victims disfigured or dead.

No immunity

When the Spanish and other Europeans arrived in Central and South America in the 15th century they brought with them a secret 'weapon'. These *conquistadors*, or conquerors, inadvertently spread smallpox and other contagious diseases among the Aztecs of Mexico and Incas of Peru. These peoples had never been exposed to the plagues and pestilences of Europe and, lacking any natural immunity, died in their millions. By the 16th century they had been wiped out, their empires disappearing forever. A century or so later the native peoples of North America suffered a similar fate. Today, isolated tribes in tropical forests are vulnerable to diseases brought in by outsiders.

Death in London

Plague disappeared and reappeared after the Black Death, most notably in London in 1665. In the hot, humid summer of that year, tens of thousands perished, dying a painful death. The plague also spread outside London. When it struck the small Derbyshire village of Eyam, its inhabitants decided, in an act of self-sacrifice, to isolate themselves to stop the epidemic spreading further.

Go further...

Follow the trail of the Black Death at:
www.abc.net.au/science/features/blackdeath/default.htm

Discover more about the *conquistadors* at:
www.pbs.org/conquistadors

Find out more about the Great Plague of London at:
www.channel4.com/history/microsites/H/history/plague/story.html

The Black Death and other Putrid Plagues of London by Natasha Narayan (Watling St, 2002)

Eyewitness – Medieval Life by Andrew Langley (Dorling Kindersley, 2000)

Biomedical scientist
Carries out research into the science of health and disease.

Biostatistician
Analyzes medical data in order to understand the distribution and spread of disease within society.

Epidemiologist
Studies diseases and how they are, or were, transmitted through people.

Medical historian
Studies the history of medicine and disease.

Zoologist
Biologist who specializes in the study of animals – including rats and fleas.

To understand more about the history of native Americans, visit:
National Museum of the American Indian, Fourth Street and Independence Avenue, SW Washington, DC 20560, USA
Telephone: +1 202 633 1000
(Also in New York, NY and Suitland, MD; see www.nmai.si.edu for details)

To find out more about what happened in Eyam in 1665–66 visit:
The Eyam Museum,
Hawkhill Road, Eyam,
Derbyshire S32 5QP, UK
Telephone: +44 (0)1433 631371
www.eyammuseum.demon.co.uk

CHAPTER 3

Old and new

There is no doubt that, in terms of public health and medicine, we have made great advances in the past 150 years. If we had been living in the mid-1800s, we would have been aware of the possibility of death by a deadly disease. Today, infectious diseases are no longer the major killers in the West. But in the developing world TB, malaria and new arrivals, such as AIDS, are killing millions. Fortunately, most of these diseases are preventable, and with appropriate action a real difference can be made in the next few years. But we should not be complacent. With new diseases arising, and more deadly or drug-resistant forms of old pathogens on the increase, the threat of epidemics is ever-present wherever in the world we live. The problems will not go away. The challenge for science is to find solutions to them.

Health workers in Hong Kong monitor an outbreak of a new viral disease – Severe Acute Respiratory Syndrome (SARS) – in 2003.

White death

Tuberculosis (TB) is an ancient disease with many names. These include 'white death' – because sufferers appear so pale – and 'consumption' – because untreated TB causes a person to waste away, or be 'consumed'. TB is caused by the bacterium *Mycobacterium tuberculosis*. It usually affects the lungs, and is spread by droplets through the air. It was a major killer in the developed world in the 19th century, and remains so today in the developing world.

City life

Throughout history, TB epidemics have surged through human societies only to recede then reappear. A new, virulent form of TB that affected the lungs appeared at the same time as the industrialization of Western cities in the 18th and 19th centuries. Aided by cramped, filthy living conditions, TB was killing millions of people each year, causing one in four deaths in London and New York.

◀ Photographed around 1890, a family pose on the steps of their home in the slums of an English city. Poverty, cramped accommodation, poor diet and inadequate health care provided ideal conditions for the spread of TB.

▲ Whole families could be wiped out by TB. This is a portrait of the Brontë sisters – English novelists – from left to right, Anne, Emily and Charlotte. Anne (1820–49) and Emily (1818–48) both died from TB, as did, most probably, the pregnant 38-year-old Charlotte in 1855.

Treating TB

Following the discovery of new antibiotic drugs in 1946, the number of TB cases in the US, UK and other developed countries fell. But since the 1980s, TB cases have been on the increase again, especially in larger cities such as New York. In the developing world, TB kills 2 million people each year. The Stop TB campaign, which started in 2006, aims to develop new treatments to make sure there are far fewer TB sufferers by 2015.

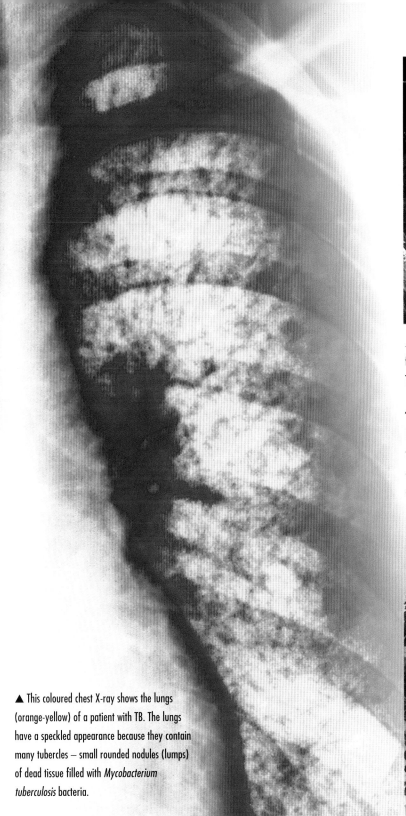

▲ This coloured chest X-ray shows the lungs (orange-yellow) of a patient with TB. The lungs have a speckled appearance because they contain many tubercles – small rounded nodules (lumps) of dead tissue filled with *Mycobacterium tuberculosis* bacteria.

Killer consumption

TB bacteria infect the lungs, damaging their tissues and affecting breathing. If untreated, they spread to other parts of the body, eventually causing wasting and death. The disease claimed the lives of millions. Most of us, if tracing our family history, are likely to find ancestors who died from consumption. By the 20th century the disease had started to recede as living conditions improved.

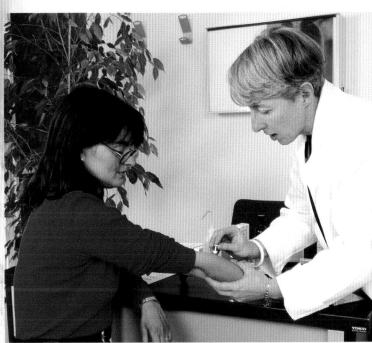

▲ A health worker is given a skin test to see if she needs to be vaccinated against TB. Vaccination is no longer routine in developed countries except for those most at risk of infection. But in the developing world vaccination is key to ending the epidemic so a new, more effective vaccine is being developed.

Pandemic panic

▲ This 1866 cartoon is called 'Death's dispensary'. By showing 'Death' pumping water for the poor, it criticizes those in power for allowing people to drink water even though there was a strong suspicion that it spread cholera.

In 1817, a disease new to the West emerged from India. It was cholera, a frightening illness spread by contaminated water and food. It caused fever, terrible diarrhoea and vomiting, and, for many of its victims, death. During the 19th century, several cholera pandemics (worldwide epidemics) caused panic and death across Asia, Europe and the Americas. Cholera still remains a threat in some parts of the world today.

Westward spread

It was the second cholera pandemic that brought the disease to Europe in 1831. Like so many diseases, cholera was believed to be the result of breathing in miasmas, or bad air, despite the fact that it affected the digestive system. Carried by European immigrants sailing to North America, cholera arrived in Montreal and New York in 1832. But this second pandemic was not the last.

▼ During the second cholera pandemic (1826–37) the disease struck Europe and the Americas for the first time. This map shows the spread of the disease from its source, in India, through Asia, Europe and then by boat to North America, spreading from there to Central and South America and the Caribbean.

▶ Unusually heavy rainfall caused this flood in Dhaka, Bangladesh, in 2004. Across the country millions of people were left homeless and at risk from epidemics of water-borne diseases such as cholera, spread when drinking water is contaminated with raw sewage.

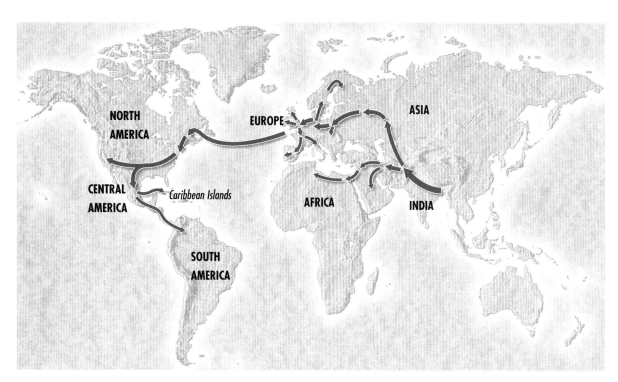

NORTH AMERICA

EUROPE

ASIA

CENTRAL AMERICA

Caribbean Islands

AFRICA

INDIA

SOUTH AMERICA

Removing the pump handle

When cholera struck once again in Britain in 1853–54, its cause was still unknown. Some 700 people died in overcrowded Soho, a district of London. English doctor John Snow (1813–58) discovered the deaths were clustered around one particular drinking water pump. Suspecting the water was contaminated, he suggested removing the pump's handle so that people could not use it. The epidemic stopped three days later.

Cholera today

Thanks to Snow's research and Koch's discovery (see page 10) we know what causes cholera and how it operates. But cholera is still a threat in parts of Asia, Africa and South America where sanitation and healthcare are poor. Cholera outbreaks often occur after natural disasters such as earthquakes or floods, when bacteria-laden sewage pollutes drinking water.

► Moved by its tail-like flagellum, this bacterium is *Vibrio cholerae*, the cause of cholera. Identified by bacteriologist Robert Koch in 1883, it releases toxins (poisons) that target and inflame the intestines, causing severe diarrhoea. Untreated, this can result in dehydration and death.

Building sewers

A growing realization that poverty, filthy living conditions and ill-health were linked inspired reformers such as Britain's Edwin Chadwick (1800–90) to force change. In cities, networks of sewers were built to help clean up the water. The sewers carried the sewage to treatment plants that processed the waste, removing germs. Clean drinking water was then piped direct to homes.

◀ This satirical engraving by William Heath (1795–1840) and dated 1828 is titled 'Monster Soup commonly called Thames Water'. It attacks the water companies for supplying Londoners with filthy drinking water filled with tiny organisms, which these strange, imaginary creatures represent.

▼ This 19th-century drawing shows a sewer being built under London's Fleet Street. Sewer construction was a massive project that helped prevent water supplies from being contaminated, and allowed people to have safe, clean water.

Public health

In the 19th century, towns and cities expanded massively as people flooded in, searching for work. Most lived in overcrowded slums with polluted water supplies, primitive sewers and little health care. Conditions were ideal for epidemics of cholera, typhoid, typhus and smallpox. Life expectancy plummeted to an all-time low. By the 1860s, cities in the USA and Britain were forced to take action to improve public health.

Filthy water

In cities and towns, water for drinking was drawn from the same rivers into which raw sewage flowed. This sewage contaminated the water with the bacteria that cause cholera and typhoid. However, a direct link between germs and diseases had yet to be made. London's River Thames was so polluted that in the summer of 1858 the 'Great Stink' drove Members of Parliament out of the House of Commons, situated close by the river.

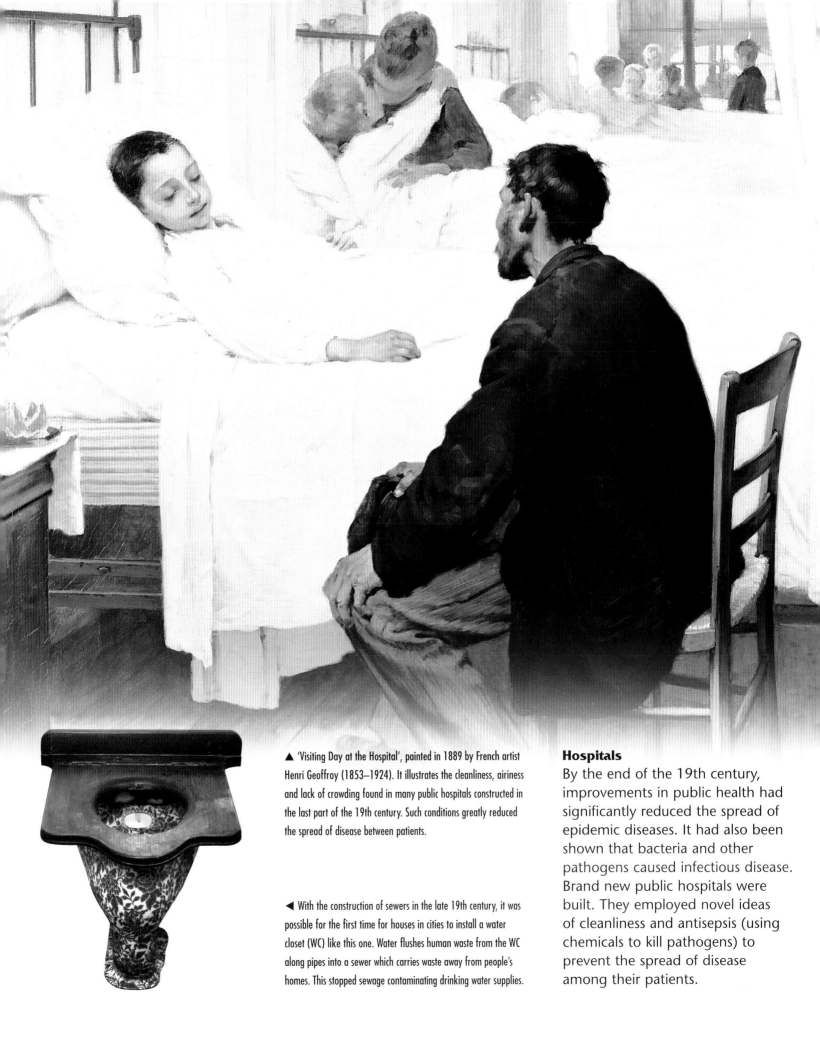

▲ 'Visiting Day at the Hospital', painted in 1889 by French artist Henri Geoffroy (1853–1924). It illustrates the cleanliness, airiness and lack of crowding found in many public hospitals constructed in the last part of the 19th century. Such conditions greatly reduced the spread of disease between patients.

◄ With the construction of sewers in the late 19th century, it was possible for the first time for houses in cities to install a water closet (WC) like this one. Water flushes human waste from the WC along pipes into a sewer which carries waste away from people's homes. This stopped sewage contaminating drinking water supplies.

Hospitals

By the end of the 19th century, improvements in public health had significantly reduced the spread of epidemic diseases. It had also been shown that bacteria and other pathogens caused infectious disease. Brand new public hospitals were built. They employed novel ideas of cleanliness and antisepsis (using chemicals to kill pathogens) to prevent the spread of disease among their patients.

Endemic diseases

An endemic disease is one that is regularly found among people in a certain area. In the developing world there are several endemic diseases caused by parasites – such as malaria, schistosomiasis and river blindness – that are largely unknown in the developed world. Left untreated, these endemic parasitic diseases make people more prone to other diseases, and reduce both their life expectancy and chances of prosperity.

Malaria
Every 30 seconds malaria kills a child in Africa. That terrifying statistic – plus the fact that malaria causes 300 million illnesses annually – underlines the threat posed by a single-celled parasite called *Plasmodium* that is spread by blood-feeding mosquitoes. Following infection a person has chills and fever, but can be treated using drugs if they are available. If not, the disease may return or even cause death.

▲ Children in Zimbabwe, Africa, are taught about the dangers of malaria. They are standing next to stagnant water, which is the perfect place for the mosquito that spreads the malaria parasite to lay its eggs.

▼ A mosquito net like this one keeps mosquitoes away from people sleeping underneath it, but allows air to circulate on hot nights. The net should not touch a person's body and should be tucked under a mattress, to ensure the mosquitoes cannot come into contact with human flesh.

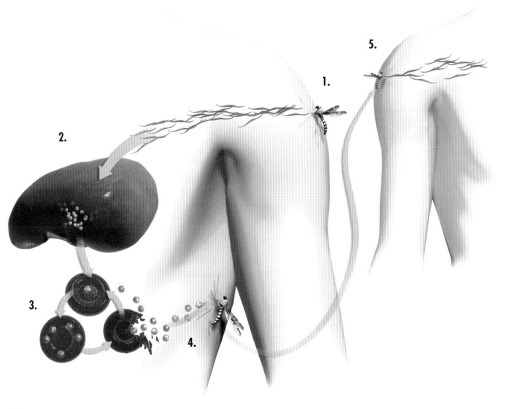

◄ Malaria is spread by mosquitoes. An infected female mosquito introduces *Plasmodium* malaria parasites into a person (1) as she feeds on blood. The parasites multiply in the liver (2) and red blood cells (3). When they burst out of red blood cells they cause fever. An uninfected mosquito (4) picks up malaria parasites during a blood meal, and passes them on to an uninfected person (5), giving them malaria.

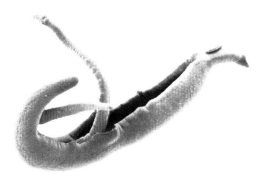

▲ This SEM shows a female schistosome worm (pink) – which lays eggs continuously – living inside the grooved body of a male worm (blue). Paired worms live in blood vessels and cause the disease schistosomiasis, or bilharzia.

Blood worms

Schistosomiasis, or bilharzia, affects 200 million people in Africa, Asia and South America. It is caused by parasitic flatworms that live in blood vessels around the bladder or intestines. The female worm lays eggs, and many remain trapped in the body, causing tissue damage. Those that pass out in urine or faeces hatch in freshwater, releasing swimming larvae that burrow into people's skin to complete the worms' life cycle. Most sufferers have no access to the drugs that could cure the disease.

River blindness

So-called because it is spread by blackflies that breed in rivers, river blindness is an endemic disease caused by parasitic roundworms. Biting blackflies introduce roundworm larvae into a person's bloodstream. These mature, mate and produce micro-worms that are attacked by the immune system. When this happens in the eyes it can cause blindness. Major programs to eliminate blackflies and kill worms using drugs have reduced the incidence of the disease.

▼ A boy uses a stick to lead a blind man through their West African village. The man's blindness was caused by river blindness, the world's second leading infectious cause of blindness, after the disease trachoma, a scarring of the cornea (front of the eye) caused by *Chlamydia* bacteria.

Colds and flu

Each winter brings with it fresh epidemics of colds and flu. Both diseases are caused by viruses, and both affect the upper part of the respiratory (breathing) system. Colds usually cure themselves. But for some people, flu can be more serious. Those most at risk, such as the elderly, should protect themselves each autumn with a flu vaccination. Pneumonia is a serious lung infection that can be triggered by colds or flu.

Common cold

Most people have experienced the sore, runny, stuffy nose that is typical of the common cold. Colds can be caused by over 100 different viruses. These viruses multiply inside nose and throat cells, then burst out of those cells ready to infect other ones. The body's response to virus infection produces thick mucus in the nose and causes coughing and sneezing, which can spread droplets containing cold viruses to other people.

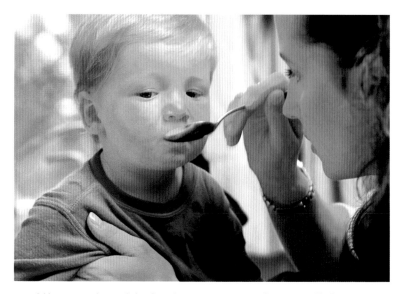

▲ A child is given medicine to help relieve the symptoms, or signs, of a common cold. These symptoms include a runny, blocked nose, a sore throat, a higher temperature than usual, and feeling feverish and generally unwell. Flu has similar symptoms but is more serious.

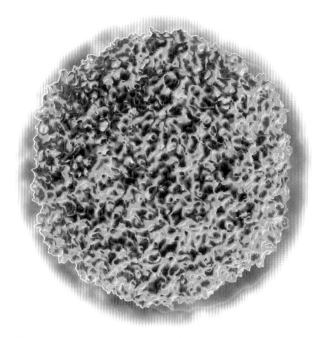

▲ This is the outside view of a rhinovirus, a member of a group of viruses that are the most common cause of colds. Spread through the air in droplets, the virus invades cells in the nose and throat, where it reproduces.

Influenza

Also spread by sneezes and coughs, flu, or influenza, is more severe than a cold, causing high fever, headache, tiredness and muscle aches. Like a cold, flu is usually eventually defeated by the body's immune system. But for people with weakened defences – such as the elderly – it can be more serious. Luckily, they can be protected by annual vaccination. Flu viruses constantly change into slightly different forms, so new vaccines are produced for each flu 'season' to target new strains.

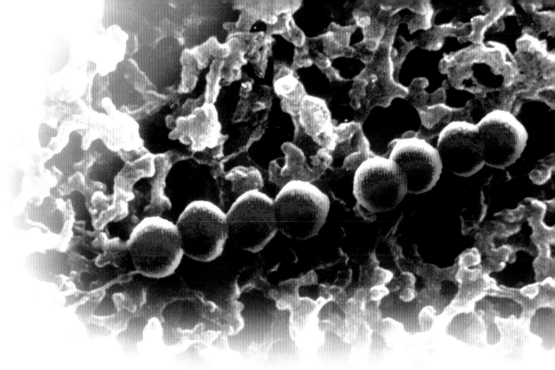

▲ A short chain of rounded *Streptococcus pneumoniae* bacteria attached to human lung tissue. Although they can live harmlessly in the body, these bacteria can cause pneumonia infections, especially in people who have weakened immune systems.

Pneumonia

Lungs are vitally important because they pull life-giving oxygen into the body. Pneumonia is an inflammation of the lungs. It reduces their efficiency, causing chest pain, fever, shortness of breath and coughing. Caused by bacteria, viruses or other pathogens, pneumonia often affects people with weakened immune (defence) systems who have recently had a cold or flu. Treating pneumonia depends on its cause and severity. Bacterial pneumonia can be treated with antibiotics. Patients with severe pneumonia may need to go into hospital for treatment.

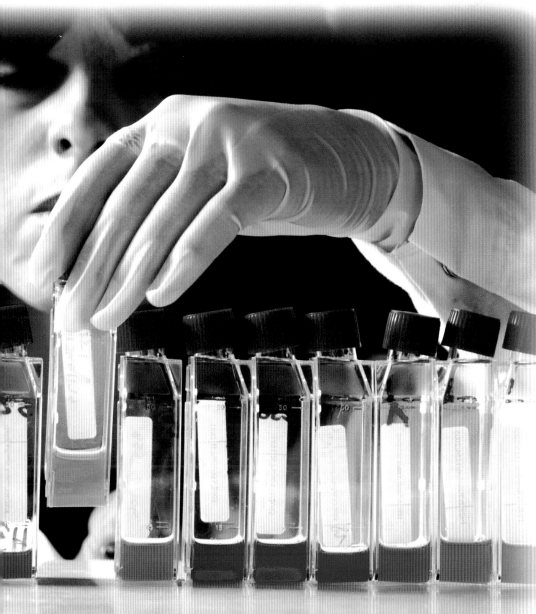

◄ A researcher checks culture flasks containing samples of flu viruses that have recently infected people. The most commonly occurring strains, or forms, of the virus will be used to make vaccine for the next flu 'season'.

Fatal flu

Annual epidemics of flu affect lots of people, most of whom fight off the virus within a few weeks. But every so often a new subtype, or form, of flu virus appears to which no-one is immune. When this happened in 1918 it caused a pandemic – a worldwide epidemic – that killed millions of people. The 1918 pandemic started in birds, not in people. A similar pandemic may be about to happen today. If it does, the source will once again be bird flu.

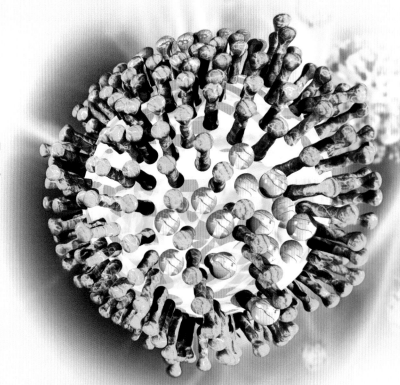

▲ This computer model shows a flu virus, in this case the H5N1 strain of avian flu. Sticking out from the coat of the virus are surface proteins that attach the virus to cells and enable virus particles to escape from cells after they have multiplied.

▲ Taken in October 1918, this photograph shows office workers wearing surgical-style face masks to help protect them from breathing in infected droplets and developing possibly fatal flu. Such masks were a common sight in 1918–19, as people carried on their daily lives in the face of the epidemic.

The 1918 pandemic

When World War I ended in 1918, some 15 million soldiers had died. But as surviving soldiers returned home, many fell prey to the deadly flu pandemic that swept the world from 1918–19 and killed over 50 million people. The virus targeted younger adults, between the ages of 25 and 40. Its first symptoms were the same as any other flu, but then, instead of recovering, patients got worse, developing severe lung problems that often proved fatal.

Avian flu

Bird, or avian, flu affects chickens, turkeys and ducks and also migratory wildfowl such as geese. There are several different subtypes of the avian flu virus. Over time, viruses change their identity, sometimes giving rise to more dangerous forms. This happened with the highly contagious H5N1 subtype, which since 1997 has caused deadly poultry epidemics in Southeast Asia. What makes H5N1 more worrying, however, is that it has caused severe disease in a few people.

▶ Anti-flu drugs greatly reduce the effects of flu. They bind to virus particles and prevent them from emerging from the cells in which they have multiplied. This stops viruses spreading to, and infecting, other cells so halting the progress of the disease.

75 mg

Future pandemic?

Scientists have now reconstructed the 1918 virus and identified it as a subtype of bird flu that appeared in poultry. The virus mutated, or changed, and became highly infectious to humans. The concern today is that H5N1 might also mutate to produce a new, dangerous strain to which humans have no immunity, that passes easily from person to person, and which will cause a new pandemic. Only when that new strain appears will scientists be able to produce a vaccine against it. In the meantime, governments are building up stocks of anti-flu drugs and researching vaccines.

◀ Vaccination of chickens and other domesticated birds against bird flu, and keeping them indoors away from migrating wild birds, may help prevent the spread of the disease. Another measure might be to slaughter whole flocks in areas where bird flu has occurred.

Beating smallpox

Smallpox, a highly contagious and dangerous viral disease, was first recorded in ancient Egypt in 1350BCE. For thousands of years, smallpox epidemics posed a deadly threat, claiming the lives of millions of people and leaving countless others scarred for life. But the discovery of vaccination in the late 18th century marked a turning point. By the end of the 1970s, smallpox had been wiped out, the first disease to be eradicated by human action.

Disfiguring disease

Passed from person to person by droplets in coughs and sneezes, smallpox spread like wildfire. A week or two after infection, victims experienced fever, headaches and a skin rash that developed eventually into pus-filled pustules. If a person survived this long – and over one-third did not – the crusty scabs that formed on the pustules fell off, leaving behind disfiguring scars.

▲ Photographed in the 1970s, this African boy clearly shows the signs of smallpox infection, his arms and face covered by highly infectious pustules. The last case of smallpox occurred in Somalia, Africa, in 1977.

Jenner's discovery

By the 18th century, smallpox had become the most serious infectious disease in the western world. But in 1796 British doctor Edward Jenner (1749–1823) made a dramatic breakthrough. He had heard that milkmaids who had contracted a mild disease called cowpox never caught smallpox. He took pus from a cowpox pustule and scraped it with a pointed blade, or lancet, into the skin of a young boy. Six weeks later, Jenner tried to infect the boy with smallpox, but he did not catch the disease.

◄ Edward Jenner vaccinates a young child against smallpox. He is scraping pus from a cowpox pustule into the child's arm using a lancet.

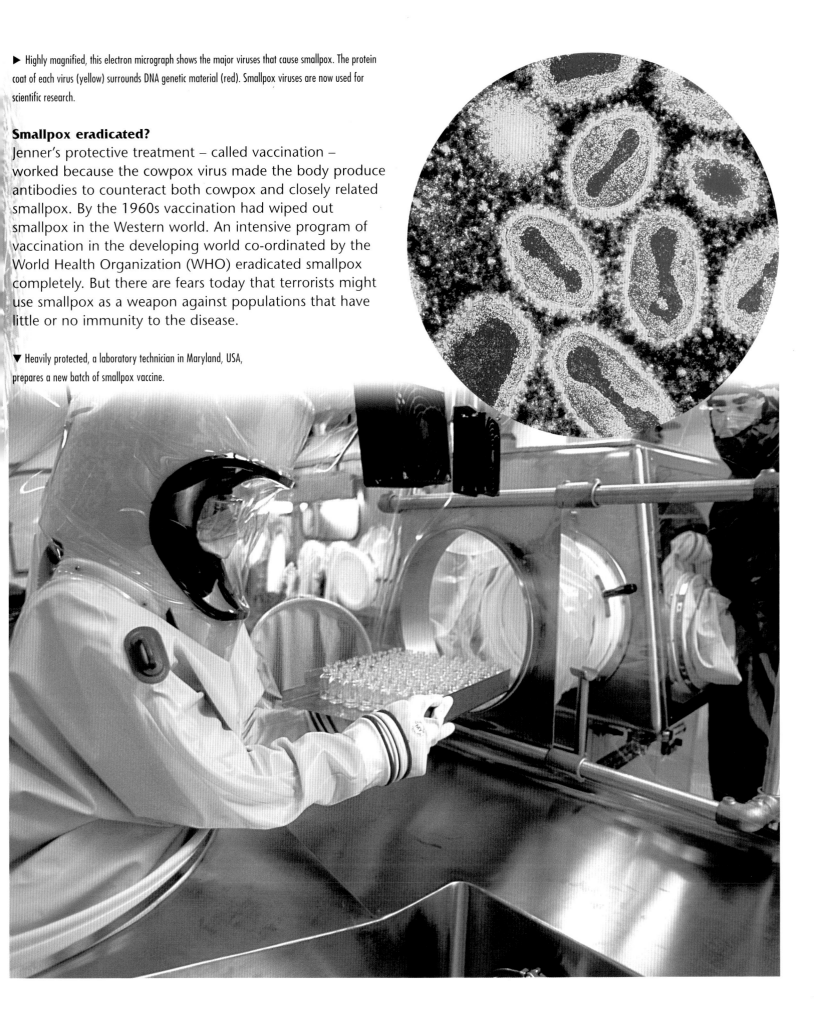

▶ Highly magnified, this electron micrograph shows the major viruses that cause smallpox. The protein coat of each virus (yellow) surrounds DNA genetic material (red). Smallpox viruses are now used for scientific research.

Smallpox eradicated?

Jenner's protective treatment – called vaccination – worked because the cowpox virus made the body produce antibodies to counteract both cowpox and closely related smallpox. By the 1960s vaccination had wiped out smallpox in the Western world. An intensive program of vaccination in the developing world co-ordinated by the World Health Organization (WHO) eradicated smallpox completely. But there are fears today that terrorists might use smallpox as a weapon against populations that have little or no immunity to the disease.

▼ Heavily protected, a laboratory technician in Maryland, USA, prepares a new batch of smallpox vaccine.

▼ This biohazard (biological hazard) symbol is recognized all around the world. It indicates that inside a marked container or package there is biological material – including, perhaps, live pathogens – that might prove harmful to human health.

Germ warfare

For centuries, germ or biological warfare has been used to kill or injure both soldiers and civilians. It involves the deliberate use of highly contagious pathogens – such as those that cause plague, smallpox or anthrax – as epidemic-producing weapons. The stockpiling and use of bioweapons was outlawed by the 1972 Biological Weapons Convention. But because of bioterrorism, germ warfare remains a real threat.

Catapulting plague

History is littered with incidents of germ warfare. Wells have been poisoned with dead animals to infect enemy forces. Native Americans may have been deliberately infected with smallpox (see page 33). But the most bizarre incident was in 1346 when soldiers besieging the Crimean port of Kaffa catapulted the bodies of plague victims into the city. Terrified, the city's occupants fled to Italy, taking the Black Death to Europe (see page 26).

▶ Medieval soldiers use a trebuchet to attack a city. This acts like a giant sling to launch large stones that will demolish walls. At Kaffa, trebuchets were used to hurl dead bodies into the city.

Twentieth-century warfare

During the 20th century, germ warfare was used by various armies throughout the world. The Japanese used bio-weapons against the Chinese during World War II. In the 1980s, the USSR is alleged to have used germ weapons in Afghanistan. Warfare itself increases the possibility of epidemic disease. The appalling conditions in the trenches of World War I led to epidemics of trench fever, a bacterial disease spread by body lice.

Bioterrorism

Today, several countries are believed to have secret germ warfare programs despite having signed up to the Biological Weapons Convention. More worryingly, bioweapons could be used by small groups of terrorists whose aim is to destabilize legitimate governments. Bioterrorists could cause panic and many deaths by releasing potentially deadly pathogens, such as smallpox or anthrax, in highly populated areas.

▼ Wearing protective clothing, three workers who deal with hazardous materials emerge from senate offices in Washington, DC, USA, in November 2001. They have been testing for anthrax spores after the discovery of a letter contaminated with anthrax that was sent to a senator.

▲ Taken in 1917, this photograph shows a British soldier sitting in a trench eating his rations during World War I. Conditions in the trenches were appalling and front-line soldiers suffered from epidemics of trench fever and other diseases.

▲ This SEM shows part of the surface of a lymphocyte (blue) – one of the body's defence cells (see pages 14–15) – taken from a person who is HIV-positive. Emerging from the lymphocyte are HIV particles (pink). Having multiplied inside the lymphocyte, these viruses will infect other cells.

HIV and AIDS

In 1981 a new, incurable condition appeared, called AIDS. Its victims developed diseases that were not normally serious but became life-threatening because their immune systems were severely weakened. In 1983 HIV, the virus that causes AIDS, was discovered. Today, some 40 million people, including 2.3 million children, are infected with HIV, and 3 million die annually from AIDS. Research continues to find a cure for the HIV pandemic.

HIV

The human immunodeficiency virus (HIV) passes from person to person in body fluids – through sexual contact, contaminated blood or between mother and baby. Everyday contact, such as through kissing or touching, cannot spread the virus. Once inside the body, HIV invades white blood cells called CD4 lymphocytes that play a key role in the body's immune system. The virus reproduces inside the lymphocyte, destroying it in the process.

A selection of the drugs used to combat HIV and help prevent AIDS. These drugs do not cure HIV, but can keep people healthy for many years by slowing the reproduction of HIV inside the body.

What is AIDS?

Over a period of years, HIV seriously weakens a person's immune system. An HIV-positive (HIV-infected) person is prey to diseases that their immune system would normally destroy. These diseases – known collectively as AIDS or acquired immunodeficiency syndrome – overwhelm the body, resulting in death. Anti-HIV drugs are now available that slow the progress of HIV, giving HIV-positive individuals hope for the future.

◄ Being fed at a hospital in South Africa, these children are orphans whose parent or parents died from AIDS. Many are HIV-positive, having been infected by their mothers.

Raising awareness

Ninety-five per cent of HIV-positive adults and children live in the developing world, many in Africa. Few have access to anti-HIV drugs and, untreated, most die from AIDS. Started in 1988, World AIDS Day aims to raise awareness about HIV and AIDS. Researchers world-wide are searching for new, more effective drugs and possibly, one day, a vaccine against this devastating virus.

NORTH AMERICA

EUROPE

ASIA

SOUTH AMERICA

AFRICA

AUSTRALIA

◄ ▲ Chinese students (left) wave flags on World AIDS Day to raise awareness about the disease. The map (above) shows red ribbons – worn as a symbol of support for AIDS prevention. The ribbons cover all the world's countries, highlighting the pandemic nature of the disease.

◀ Wearing protective clothing, health workers in a village in the Democratic Republic of the Congo in Africa investigate an outbreak of Ebola fever. Although at high risk of infection, health workers isolate Ebola patients and stabilize their condition to increase their chance of survival.

Future epidemics

The belief that modern science can prevent new epidemic diseases from arising, or immediately find a cure for any that do appear, is false. Some new diseases, such as Ebola fever, appear when pathogens change, allowing them to move from animals to humans. Others, such as vCJD, arise because of human activity. A few, including West Nile disease, have spread to new places through air travel.

Ebola fever

The virus that causes Ebola fever is one of the most destructive and lethal known to humankind. Since its discovery in central Africa in 1976 there have been several outbreaks. Symptoms include fever and severe bleeding. Ebola strikes so rapidly that many victims die before their immune system has time to respond. The virus is also highly contagious, passing from person to person by direct contact.

BSE and vCJD

The epidemic of bovine spongiform encephalopathy (BSE) first appeared in herds of British cattle in 1986. They had been fed on carcasses of sheep that had died from a brain-destroying disease called scrapie. Both BSE and scrapie are caused by an infective agent called a prion. Since 1996, some people have been struck down by a new, incurable brain disease called variant Creutzfeld-Jacob disease (vCJD). They contracted the disease by eating beef products containing the prion that caused BSE.

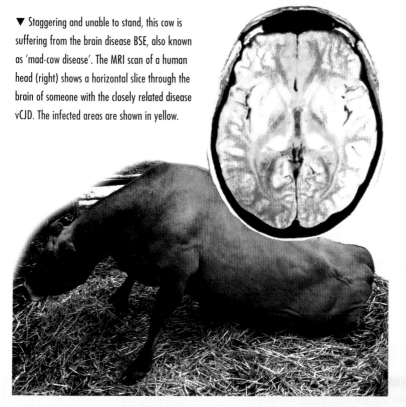

▼ Staggering and unable to stand, this cow is suffering from the brain disease BSE, also known as 'mad-cow disease'. The MRI scan of a human head (right) shows a horizontal slice through the brain of someone with the closely related disease vCJD. The infected areas are shown in yellow.

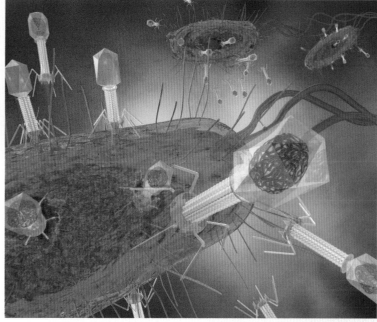

▲ These are bacteriophages – viruses that attack bacteria. They inject genetic material inside the bacterium to create more copies of themselves, killing the bacterium in the process. In the future, bacteriophages may be used to target and destroy bacteria that cause human diseases.

West Nile disease

First identified in Uganda, Africa, in 1937, West Nile Virus arrived in New York in 1999. The disease was probably introduced by an air passenger, and it soon spread across North and Central America. Caused by a virus related to yellow fever virus, the disease affects mainly birds. It is transmitted to humans by blood-feeding mosquitoes. In most cases it causes mild flu-like symptoms, but if the virus enters the brain it can cause death.

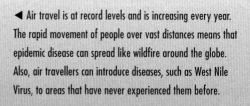

◀ Air travel is at record levels and is increasing every year. The rapid movement of people over vast distances means that epidemic disease can spread like wildfire around the globe. Also, air travellers can introduce diseases, such as West Nile Virus, to areas that have never experienced them before.

New challenges, new treatments

The widespread use of antibiotics and other pathogen-killing drugs has dramatically reduced the death toll from epidemic diseases. But now there are many strains of drug-resistant pathogens, so that, in future, new treatments will be needed to fight diseases. Possible solutions include making genetically engineered antibodies that target specific viruses. Another method is to use viruses – called bacteriophages – that kill bacteria.

SUMMARY OF CHAPTER 3: OLD AND NEW

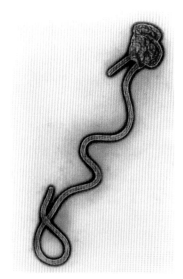

This single Ebola virus resembles a coiled wire.

Then and now

In 19th century Europe and North America, cities expanded rapidly. Many people lived in crowded housing and were without adequate sanitation. These conditions provided the ideal environment for epidemics of killer diseases such as TB and cholera. But in the second half of the century the links between poverty, 'germs' and disease were beginning to be discovered. Public health reforms, such as the provision of clean drinking water, helped improve health and this led to a decline in infectious diseases. The story in the developing world is different, however, because of poor living conditions and a lack of adequate health care. Here TB and other epidemic diseases are still major killers.

Flu threat

The common cold – a mild, infectious disease that is familiar world-wide – is usually defeated by the body's immune (defence) system within a few days. Colds are caused by viruses and spread by sneezes and coughs. The same is true of influenza, or flu, a more serious infection of the respiratory (breathing) system that can kill those people who have weakened immune systems. Sometimes a deadlier form of flu virus arises. Such a virus caused a pandemic in 1918–19 that killed millions. That threat still exists today.

The end of disease?

Smallpox was once a deadly viral disease that scarred those it did not kill. It has now been wiped out. Does this mean that other diseases can be eradicated so that epidemics become a thing of the past? Unfortunately, no. New diseases, such as AIDS and Ebola fever, arise, usually when animal pathogens alter and become capable of infecting humans. While science cannot eradicate all diseases, it can work to control old ones and deal with new infections as they arise.

Go further...

Find out about John Snow, cholera and other epidemic diseases at: www.makingthe modernworld.org.uk/learning_module s/geography/05.TU.01/?section=2

See letters and photos relating to the 1918 influenza epidemic in the USA at: www.archives.gov/exhibits/influenza-epidemic/index.html

Read the full story about the eradication of smallpox at: www.bbc.co.uk/history/discovery/medicine/smallpox_01.shtml

Eyewitness – Epidemic by Brian Ward (Dorling Kindersley, 2000)

Environmental engineer
Improves public health by providing clean water and air to human habitations.

Environmental health inspector
Enforces public health regulations, thereby preventing the spread of disease and promoting good health.

International health specialist
Public health practitioner whose work focuses on improving health in developing countries.

Parasitologist
Studies the life cycle, structure and biochemistry of parasites, including those that cause diseases in humans.

Visit the Edward Jenner Museum (situated in the house that was Jenner's home) to find out more about Jenner, vaccination and immunology:
The Edward Jenner Museum, Berkeley, Gloucestershire GL13 9BH, UK
Telephone: +44 (0)1453 810631
www.jennermuseum.com

Discover the history of public health by visiting:
The Museum of Science & Industry in Manchester, Liverpool Road, Castlefield, Manchester M3 4FP, UK
Telephone: +44 (0)161 832 2244
www.msim.org.uk/index.asp?menuid=723

Glossary

anthrax
A bacterial disease that affects the skin and lungs of cattle and humans.

antibiotic
A drug, such as penicillin, that is used to kill, or slow the growth of, disease-causing bacteria.

Aztecs
Native Americans who established an empire in central Mexico between the 14th and 16th centuries CE.

bacteria (singular bacterium)
A group of microscopic, single-celled organisms, some of which cause disease in humans.

bioterrorism
The use of pathogens as weapons by terrorists.

blight
A group of diseases that affect plants and may be caused by fungi, bacteria or viruses.

CDC (Centers for Disease Control and Prevention)
A US agency responsible for protecting public health.

cell
One of the microscopic living units from which all organisms are made.

Christopher Columbus
An Italian-born explorer (1451–1506) who was the first European to reach the Americas in 1492.

contagious
Describes a disease, such as measles, that passes easily from person to person.

deer mouse
A type of mouse found in North America.

deficiency disease
A disease caused by the shortage of a vitamin, mineral or other nutrient in a person's diet.

dementia
A severe decline in a person's memory, thinking and other brain skills, caused by disease.

disease
An illness caused by a malfunction in one or more body systems.

endemic
Describes a disease that is always present in certain groups of people or particular locations.

epidemic
An outbreak of an infectious disease that affects many people in the same place at one time.

epidemiology
The study of the cause and distribution of diseases in a population.

fungi (singular fungus)
A group of organisms that are neither animals nor plants (eg. mushrooms and moulds). Some fungi cause disease.

gangrene
The death of part of the body, such as a finger, caused by infection or lack of blood supply.

genetic material
The molecules of DNA found inside cells that carry the instructions (genes) needed to construct and run an organism.

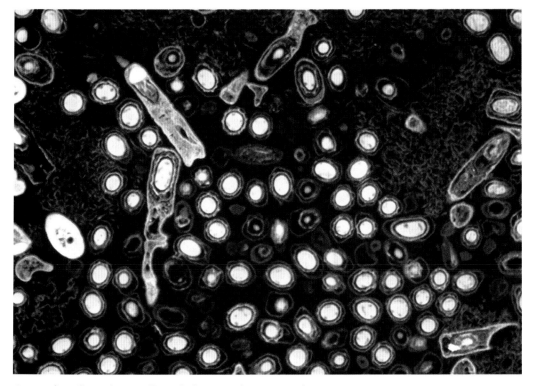

Spores of *Bacillus anthracis* (yellow), the bacterium that causes anthrax.

genome

A complete set of genes (instructions) found inside a cell of a living organism.

germ

A general term for a micro-organism that causes disease.

Global Polio Eradication Initiative

A partnership set up by a group of international organizations in 1988 to eradicate polio world-wide.

haemorrhagic

Describes a disease that causes severe bleeding or haemorrhaging.

hallucination

Seeing or hearing things that do not really exist.

hunter-gatherer

A member of a group of people who live by hunting and gathering plants.

Ice Age

One of several periods in Earth's history when the climate was much colder than usual.

immunity

The ability of the body's immune system to protect it against specific diseases.

immunodeficiency

A state in which the immune system's ability to fight infection is greatly reduced.

Incas

Native Americans who established an empire in Peru in the 15th and 16th centuries CE.

infectious disease

A disease, such as flu, that is caused by pathogens.

lancet

A sharp surgical instrument with a double-edged blade.

lymph nodes

Small, bean-shaped swellings, also called 'glands', in which pathogens are destroyed. They may swell up during infections.

lymphocyte

A type of white blood cell that plays a key role in the immune system by recognizing and attacking pathogens.

macrophage

One type of white blood cell that tracks down and destroys pathogens.

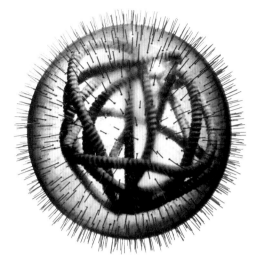

Computer model of a measles virus

medieval

Describes something relating to the Middle Ages.

mercenary

A solder who, if paid, will fight for any army.

mercury

A silvery metal that is liquid at room temperature.

miasma

A mysterious 'vapour' that was believed at one time to cause and spread disease.

micro-organism

A tiny organism, such as a bacterium, that can only be seen by using a microscope.

Middle Ages

The period of European history between the 5th and 15th centuries CE.

MRSA (*Methicillin-resistant Staphylococcus aureus*)

A pathogenic bacterium that cannot be destroyed by most antibiotics. Also called a 'superbug'.

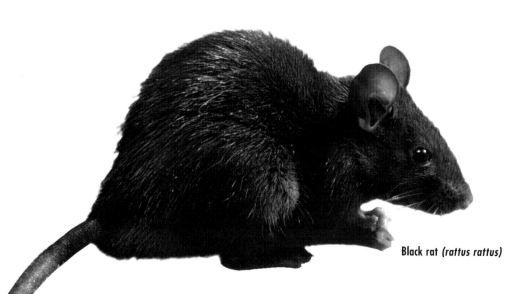

Black rat *(rattus rattus)*

mucus
Thick, slimy protective fluid secreted by the lining of the mouth, nose and other hollow organs.

Navajo
The largest native American tribe in North America.

neutrophil
One type of white blood cell that tracks down and destroys pathogens.

non-infectious disease
A disease, such as diabetes, that is not directly caused by pathogens.

obesity
A condition in which a person is severely overweight because their body has excessive fat (energy) stores.

pandemic
An epidemic of an infectious disease that spreads world-wide.

paralysis
The loss of the ability to move one or more parts of the body.

parasite
An organism that lives, feeds and reproduces in or on another organism.

pathogen
A micro-organism such as a bacterium, virus or protist that causes disease.

phagocyte
A general name for white blood cells – including neutrophils and macrophages – that engulf and destroy pathogens.

prion
An infectious agent, far simpler even than a virus, that consists of just a protein.

protist
One of a group of single-celled organisms, some of which cause disease.

pus
A yellowish-white fluid found at the site of an infection which contains many dead white blood cells that have destroyed pathogens.

rust
A microscopic fungus that causes disease in certain plants.

SEM (scanning electron micrograph)
A photograph taken using a scanning electron microscope.

Burying the dead in London, 1665

tick
A relative of spiders that sucks blood from animals and may transmit disease.

toxin
A poisonous substance produced by some pathogens, especially bacteria, that damages the organism that they infect.

trebuchet
A medieval machine used in warfare to launch stones against an enemy.

vaccination
The injection into the body of a fragment or weakened version of a pathogen in order to give protection against a specific disease. It is also called immunization.

vector
An animal, such as a fly, mosquito or bat, that carries and spreads a pathogen from person to person.

viral
Describes a disease caused by a virus.

virus
A non-living, infectious agent that causes disease when it invades body cells in order to reproduce.

vitamin
One of a group of substances needed in tiny amounts in the diet to keep the body working normally.

Index

Acknowledgements

The publisher would like to thank the following for permission to reproduce their material. Every care has been taken to trace copyright holders. However, if there have been unintentional omissions or failure to trace copyright holders, we apologize and will, if informed, endeavour to make corrections in any future edition.

Key: *b* = bottom, *c* = centre, *l* = left, *r* = right, *t* = top

Cover *l* Alamy/Stock Image; cover *c* Science Photo Library (SPL)/CNRI; cover *r* Corbis/William Whitehurst; pages 1 Frank Lane Picture Agency (FLPA)/Terry Whittaker; 2–3 SPL/CDC; 4–5 Corbis/Bettmann; 7 Bridgeman Art Library (BAL)/British Library; 8–9 Corbis/Reuters; 8*bl* Corbis/Jonathan Blair; 9*tr* Werner Forman Archive; 9*br* Corbis/Lee Snider; 10 Corbis/ Bettmann; 11*tl* SPL/Alfred Pasieka; 11*cr* SPL/CAMR; 11*br* SPL/Eye of Science; 12*tl* Photolibrary.com; 12–13 Alamy/Photo Japan; 13*t* Ardea/Nick Gordon; 13*b* SPL/Jane Shemilt; 14*tl* SPL/Eye of Science; 15*cr* Corbis/Hulton; 16*tr* Corbis/Karen Kasmauski; 16*cl* Corbis/Bettmann; 16*cr* Alamy/Phototake Inc.; 17*r* Corbis/CDC; 18*bl* Corbis/David Turnley; 18–19*t* BAL/ Brooklyn Museum of Art, New York; 19*tr* Alamy/Janine Wiedel; 19*b* Corbis/Karen Kasmauski; 20*l* Corbis/Bettmann; 20*bl* inset Photolibrary.com; 20*r* Getty/AFP; 21*t* Corbis/Liba Taylor; 21*b* Alamy/Homer Sykes; 22 BAL/Victoria Art Gallery, Bath; 23*tr* Corbis/Free Agents Ltd; 23*b* Corbis/W. Perry Conway; 24 SPL/Eye of Science; 25 SPL/Barry Dowsett; 26*b* The Art Archive/ Biblioteca Nazionale Marciana Venice/Dagli Orti; 27*tl* FLPA/Derek Middleton; 27*tl* inset SPL/Dr Tony Brain; 27*br* The Art Archive/Biblioteca Estense Modena/Dagli Orti; 28*tl* SPL/Astrid & Hanns-Frieder Michler; 28–29 The Art Archive/Biblioteca Augusta Perugia/Dagli Orti; 29*tr* Horace Howard Furness Memorial Library, University of Pennsylvania; 29*b* BAL/Private Collection; 30*cl* The Art Archive/Galleria d'Arte Moderna Florence/Dagli Orti; 30*tr* BAL/Bibliotheque Nationale France; 30–31*b* SPL/Jackie Lewin, Royal Free Hospital; 31*tr* BAL/Tretyakov Gallery, Moscow; 32*cl* Alamy/Pictorial Press; 33*bl* Corbis/ Keren Su; 33*tr* Corbis/Historical Picture Archive; 35*br* Topfoto; 36 BAL/British Library; 37 Corbis/Reuters; 38*bl* Corbis/ Hulton; 38–39 SPL/ISM; 39*t* Corbis/Sygma; 39*br* Topfoto; 40*tl* Mary Evans Picture Library; 40–41 Getty/AFP; 41*tr* SPL/ Moredun Animal Health Ltd; 42*tl* Science & Society Picture Library; 42*br* BAL/Guildhall, London; 43*t* BAL/Hotel de Ville, Vichy, France; 43*bl* National Trust, London; 44*tl* Alamy/Neil Cooper; 44*b* Corbis/Robert van der Hilst; 45*tr* SPL/NIBSC; 45*b* Empics/AP; 46*bl* SPL; 46*tr* Photolibrary.com; 46–47*b* SPL/James King-Holmes; 47*tr* SPL/BSIP; 48*cl* Corbis/Bettmann; 48–49*b* Corbis/Reuters; 49*tr* SPL; 50*bl* Wellcome Institute Picture Library; 50*tr* Corbis/Paul Almasy; 51*tr* SPL/Eye of Science; 51*b* Corbis/Karen Kasmauski; 52 Corbis/William Whitehurst; 52*bl* BAL/British Library; 53*tl* Corbis/Underwood & Underwood; 53*b* Getty/Alex Wong; 54*tl* SPL/NIBSC; 54–55 Getty/Per-Anders Pettersson; 55*t* Getty/Joe Raedle; 55*bl* Getty/Katharina Hesse; 55*br* SPL/Victor Habbick Visions; 56*t* Corbis/Sygma; 56–57 Corbis/Gunter Marx; 57*cl* inset SPL/Simon Fraser, Royal Victoria Infirmary; 57*cl* Rex Features; 57*tr* Alamy/Phototake Inc.; 58 SPL/Barry Dowsett; 59 SPL/Scott Camazine; 60*bl* FLPA/Derek Middleton; 60*tr* SPL/OMIKRON; 61 The Art Archive; 62–63 SPL/Kwangshin Kim; 64 SPL/Sinclair Stammers

The publisher would like to thank the following illustrators:
Julian Baker 26, 40; Sebastian Quigley 45; Jurgen Ziewe 14–15, 34–35

The author would like to thank Marie Greenwood for her diligence and enthusiasm, Rebecca Painter for her excellent designs, and other members of the Kingfisher team for their hard work.